ACCLAIM FOR
THE EMERGING FILM COMPOSER

"*The Emerging Film Composer* contains the kind of information that usually comes only with years of professional experience. Bellis lays out not only good working habits but discusses the all important "people skills" which help to create a pleasant and successful work environment."
—James Newton Howard,
Emmy Award winner and six time Academy Award nominee
composer: *Blood Diamond, King Kong, The Interpreter, The Village, Sixth Sense*

"*The Emerging Film Composer* is the most unique and probably—if not certainly—the most useful and practical book about composing with packages ever published. Bellis' homework, figures and conclusions are most useful. If young, would-be composers read nothing else before they hop the freight train for L.A., they should be forced to read this."
—Bruce Broughton,
Academy Award nominee and ten time Emmy Award winner
composer: *Silverado, Tombstone, The Rescuers Down Under*

"A young composer can dream about the art of composing music for motion pictures and television, and the fame that often accompanies a successful film composing career. Unfortunately, dreams alone don't pay the rent. Composer and master educator Richard Bellis has assembled a wonderful guide to dealing realistically with the business side of this seductive career. Don't lift a pencil until this book is read from cover to cover. The advice is invaluable."
—Alf Clausen, Emmy Award winner and multiple Annie Award winner
composer: *The Simpsons*

"Wonderful! Richard Bellis has produced the "missing link" for film composers. This book can immediately and positively impact the productivity, earnings, and career path of film and television composers. Bellis describes plainly those awkward and embarrassing issues that music and film schools don't teach—how to value your

work and how to explain the value to producers. Everyone planning to be a professional film composer should read this book."
—Paul Hoffert, Chair, Guild of Canadian Film Composers,
Faculty Fellow at Harvard University

"I know of no other composer who is more qualified to write a book on our industry. Richard Bellis' credits reflect his expertise in all areas of our business from film to television, music direction to theme parks. Capturing every mood from comedy to suspense, drama to horror, he has executed each with the professionalism that befits our noble craft. If his proficiency as a composer weren't enough, his ability to lead, as evidenced by his remarkable stewardship of the Society of Composers and Lyricists and his years of teaching, inspiring a generation of young composers, speak to his overall competence in imparting the wisdom contained herein. This book is insightful, to-the-point and offers a 'no nonsense, no holds barred' outlook at today's profession. It is definitely a 'must read' for anyone hoping to navigate the turbulent waters of film composition."
—Dan Foliart, President, The Society of Composers & Lyricists,
composer: *7th Heaven, Home Improvement, Roseanne*

"Richard Bellis has made tremendous contributions to composer seminars presented by the Guild of Canadian Film Composers over the years. He has all the right credentials and talents for communicating the essentials for success in film scoring. I'm reading *The Emerging Film Composer* in the mixing theater as the music, effects, and dialogue (reverse that order) find their place in the soundtrack of my current project. I can't get over how pertinent Richard's points are to everything I've just been through—again! No matter how many times one has made this trek, its massively irregular dimensions demand serious navigation and attention to detail. As an ever-emerging composer, I will keep this book open on my desk through each chapter of every project I do. To forget one point in the heat of the deadline can be costly."
—Christopher Dedrick, film composer,
President, Guild of Canadian Film Composers,
Genie Award winner and multiple Gemini Award winner

"So well expressed—so beautifully laid out—and so eloquently written. This is all about the real world of music to the screen. This is everything I have not been able to express so explicitly about what we go through as screen composers, the reality of our business, the psychology of it all, an insight to inner emotions and the process of the creative. It is honest and has great sincerity. *The Emerging Film Composer* is an absolute necessity for all involved with the art and craft of screen entertainment. This text will be so valuable for the industry—and not just for composers! But for composers it will be their bible. I thank Richard for his well-crafted work—a book that will be an essential aid to keeping the structure and dignity of our future, an asset for the upcoming screen composer."

—Art Phillips, President, The Australian Guild of Screen Composers, Councillor, Film & TV Music sector, The Music Council of Australia, composer: *Outback House* (Australian series), *Missing Persons Unit*, *The Lost Treasure of Fiji, Santa Barbara*

"...Richard Bellis uncovers and delves into the psychology of the business while addressing the multi-faceted art and craft of film scoring. His vast experiences as a composer paired with his natural abilities as a teacher make this a first-rate, personal and pragmatic work. This rare combination is one that will benefit anyone interested in pursuing a career in the film and multimedia marketplace, including directors and producers. This book is unlike any other on the subject of film scoring, and long overdue. Thank you, Richard, for delivering what I'm sure will become a standard for years to come. I will be sure to recommend this book to all of my students in the USC Film Scoring program and the USC School of Cinema."

—Brian King,
Director, Scoring for Motion Pictures and Television Program
Flora L. Thornton School of Music, University of Southern California

"This book is invaluable information for any aspiring film composer. I plan to recommend it to all my students."

—Elizabeth Sellers, Director, Commercial and Media Writing, Department of Music, California State University, Northridge

ABOUT THE AUTHOR

Richard Bellis is an Emmy Award winning composer who, for the past 20 years, has found time to teach and mentor as well as compose. He has served on the faculty of the USC Scoring for Motion Pictures and Television program and taught film scoring for UCLA Extension. He is a past president of the Society of Composers & Lyricists and has served on the board of governors for the Academy of Television Arts and Sciences. In addition, he annually mentors a select group of emerging composers for the "ASCAP Television & Film Scoring Workshop with Richard Bellis."

Mr. Bellis currently lives in Santa Barbara, California with wife Gloria, their three chickens and two beagles.

THE EMERGING
FILM COMPOSER

An Introduction to the
People, Problems and Psychology
of the Film Music Business

RICHARD BELLIS

Front cover photo of Todd-AO West: Ed Kalnins
5m4 sketch: Richard Bellis
Back cover photo of Richard Bellis: Lester Cohen/Wire Image
Cover design: Colette Briere

Illustrations by Mark Henderson

Information on purchasing additional copies of this book may be obtained at:
www.richardbellis.com

Library of Congress Control Number: 2007900898
ISBN-13: 978-0-615-13623-3
ISBN-10: 0-615-13623-0

To My Dad. The Music Teacher.
The perfect blend of Mr. Holland and Professor Harold Hill.
Dedication, Substance and Charisma.

ACKNOWLEDGMENTS

Many people have thoughts they wish to share with others. One of the more challenging ways to accomplish this is to write and publish a book. Charles Wilkinson, friend and author of *The Working Director,* created such a wonderful book that it inspired me to actually finish this one. Indispensable to this laborious process are the artistic contributions of Colette Briere-Schwartz: design, layout, copy editing and warehouse of knowledge. Thanks also to fellow composers Mark Henderson for the wonderful and whimsical illustrations and John Guth for proofreading. The final ingredients: a few words of much needed encouragement and one legendary story, came from old friend, respected author and repository of all historical information on film music, Jon Burlingame.

Virtually every thought in this book is the result of an interaction with someone. Many of whom have served as examples, some as mentors, others as enablers and a few as adversaries. Some for a matter of minutes, others for years. Teachers, students, colleagues and family—all important—all contributors. I have learned from each of the folks listed below (alphabetically):

Mark Bacino, Buddy Baker, Adrienne Bellis, Dorothy Bellis, Charles Bernstein, Elmer Bernstein, Bruce Broughton, Scott Cochran, Charles Crenshaw, John Dennis, Jim DiPasquale, Dennis Dreith, Allen Epstein, Adam Fields, Jack Fierman, Jerry Goldsmith, Jim Green, Jack Gruberman, Rob Guillory, Arthur Hamilton, Ed Kalnins, Avi Kipper, Erma Levin, Ken Lisi, Henry Mancini, Ollie Mitchell, Bob Rithauler, Dave Robertson, John Rosenberg, Michael Ryan, Stan Shpetner, Michael Todd, Tommy Lee Wallace, George Wilkins, Steve Winogradsky.

Equally important are the officers, the board and the membership of the Society of Composers & Lyricists. Certainly the ladies and gentlemen of the studio orchestras and 20 years of students deserve my gratitude as well.

Finally, the person I learn from daily—my incredible wife, Gloria.

CONTENTS

INTRODUCTION

*The emerging film composer is leaving
the warmth and comfort of the academic cocoon
for the glare and noise of the "real" world.*

Composing music for film is a great job. It's fun, it's easy and it's rewarding—until you "people" it. Writing music is a solitary occupation; writing film music often becomes a group activity. How you deal with that and a multitude of other obstacles inherent in this craft could well mean the difference between success and failure.

There are many fine books on the techniques of writing music for film and television. Additionally, you can find books on orchestration, conducting and working with electronics. *The Emerging Film Composer* deals primarily with the people, problems and psychology involved with being a film composer. While this should not be the first book you read on the subject of composing music for media, it might just be the last. That's because once we officially launch our careers, our classroom tends to become the recording studio, the dubbing stage, the filmmaker's office and our own writing studio.

Today, the community of film and television composers is divided into at least three strata. The economic reality is that while some areas of work show steadily increasing fees and budgets, other areas are reducing both fees and music production budgets and rolling those costs into package deals. A divergent economy.

Historically the "A" list pictures use about eight different composers at any given time. Occasionally we will see a new name on this list, but for the most part the scores for big budget movies revolve between the "high eight." This segment of our economic spectrum is healthy and pretty much mirrors the increases seen in overall "A" list film budgets. These music budgets can incorporate composer fees in excess of a million dollars per film with a music production budget that can easily equal that amount.

The next stratum would be the slightly more modest films in which the composer might make several hundred thousand dollars and have a budget slightly less than that fee.

My best, conservative estimate is that these two categories utilize about eight to ten percent of the media composers worldwide.

Now we take a sizable step down, financially. Composers in the remaining 90 percent work on games, movies for television, television series, theme parks, independent features (low budget), documentaries, industrial films and commercials. I will limit the discussions in this book to subjects which pertain to this group, on the assumption that emerging film composers will at least pass through this category on their way elsewhere.

I am a big fan of knowing why; why things are the way they are. I believe that frustration is directly linked to expectation. Understanding why things work the way they do is the first step in creating a strategy for success.

Why do filmmakers like the music they like? What makes them comfortable or uncomfortable when it comes time to put music in their film? How can you make them *want* to like your cues? How do you "court the muse" on a deadline? How much are you worth? Can you live on that? How can you increase your efficiency in the studio or at your writing desk? How can you get your next job while working on the current one? This book speaks to these and other, similar issues.

If life (as a film composer) is a journey, then this book is a list of rest stops, restaurants and gas stations.

Relax, grab a snack and fill up.

CHAPTER ONE

PREPARATION

*The goal is to become **almost** overqualified.*

Film composers come from a wide variety of educational and career backgrounds. Some have advanced music degrees while others don't read or write music at all. Some have been studio musicians and others come from well-known rock bands. Regardless of your background, the importance of preparedness is far greater today than ever before.

In the past 15 years the number of those claiming to be film and television composers has at least doubled and more than likely tripled. This large number of new composers makes it very easy for filmmakers, agents and studio executives to say, "Next." In other words, it's a buyer's market.

When you finally get a shot, you must be ready or it may be a long time before the next opportunity comes along.

Let's examine some of the educational paths you might find useful.

FORMAL EDUCATION

A formal music education is a wonderful thing to have; you can acquire many important compositional tools. Interestingly, we often overlook or undervalue the benefits of being required to listen to and analyze music that, left to our own devices, we would never spend time with. Since film composers seldom know what they may be called upon to recreate or in what style they may be asked to write, this background becomes your earliest musical vocabulary—your toolbox. The more extensive and widely varied, the better.

Will anyone ask you what university you attended or what degrees you hold? No.

Can you work as a film composer without a college education? Absolutely.

Many colleges and universities are currently offering film and television or media music courses. Some are considered advanced studies, others are extension courses and still others are offered to undergrads. If you are choosing a college to attend and your focus is film music, those institutions with the greatest proximity to working film composers should top your list. It is likely that those composers will be serving as teachers within those programs.

GAP-FILLING

We all have gaps in our musical education. This is an unavoidable reality due to our earliest predilection toward a specific instrument or type of music, maybe the music our parents liked. A young cellist might grow up with a wonderful background in classical music but be uncomfortable with jazz or pop. A percussionist who has no problem with complex meters may show some degree of insecurity when it comes to string voicings. A keyboard player may never have had an opportunity to work under a conductor and consequently may be reticent to write free time or rubato.

Unlike a concert composer who might receive a commission based on the style in which she writes, we may be called upon to write in any number of different genres. Often we know nothing about the musical likes and dislikes of the filmmaker until we are deep into the first meeting. At that time we may have to pull, from our proverbial hat, everything we know about 16TH century Chinese music.

Can you say *pipa?*

Gap-filling requires one to self-diagnose the gaps and create a personal curriculum for filling them. I can almost guarantee that one of the first important jobs you are offered will fall right into one of these gaps. Much like Murphy's Law, my students have come to know this as Bellis' Law.

PRIVATE STUDY

Private study allows you to focus your education specifically where you want it. You move at your own speed rather than the speed of the slowest person in class. And there is another reason to study privately. If you pick as your teacher someone active in the industry—someone you'd like to meet or whose work you admire—that person could turn out to be a mentor or resource who will benefit your career. Private study is usually too expensive for a general introduction to film scoring and consequently is most useful to the more advanced student who wants to brush up certain skills such as orchestration or conducting.

WORKSHOPS, SEMINARS, INTERNSHIPS AND MENTOR PROGRAMS

There are more workshops, internships and seminars being offered now than ever before. *(See Appendix for a partial list of programs.)* While they are packed with information and sometimes a chance to write, record and hear your work, they also offer a chance for face-to-face meetings with people who A) could be instrumental in advancing your career and B) are your peers and might be helpful when you need assistance on a project. If you are strong in electronics, you might benefit from having a friend who is an experienced orchestrator.

LEARNING OTHER PEOPLE'S JOBS

Only on the lowest budget films will a composer be the lone member of the music department. On most productions you will assemble a team of talented people with whom to work. Everyone connected with the preparation, production and delivery of the music is attempting to make you look like a hero. They are proud of their own skills and want to do the best job possible. The responsibility for these people being able to do their best work lies, at least in part, with you. To keep from inadvertently sabotaging them, you should have a working knowledge of how they do what they do.

Some examples might be:

Your *scoring mixer* will need to know in advance what the exact instrumentation for the session is going to be. Not only will the studio want to set up the right number of stands and chairs in the proper configuration, but the mixer will want to choose the mics and may need to rent additional mics or other equipment that the studio doesn't own. He will be thinking about track assignments, mic positioning, whether to take the guitars stereo or mono. There are myriad decisions to make and the more time he has, the better your music will be recorded.

The *copyist* is the one person with a more stressful deadline than yours. Her deadline is the downbeat of the session. Unless you notify her in advance that you will be delivering a four-minute cue the morning of the recording session, she may not be able to line up enough people to get the copying finished by the end of the session. In addition, while working from the score, the copyist is normally responsible for finding out what percussion instruments and other doubles might be required. She then passes that information to the players or the contractor so that they can arrange for those instruments to be at the session. Consequently, if, on the morning of the session, you turn in a cue that uses instruments not called for on any of the previous cues, you run the risk of those instruments not showing up on time.

The *music editor* can save your cue, your budget and your life (often in the form of your reputation) if you know what he can and, more importantly, cannot do. Like everyone else on the team he needs time to perform many of his tasks. You may find yourself in the inadvisable position of serving as your own music editor one day, so time spent learning about all aspects of this job is time well spent.

You should have some idea about instruments that can be physically demanding. How high, and for how long without rests, can brass players play? You don't want to find yourself standing in front of an angry trumpet section.

Another important job to study is that of the *filmmaker.* You need to know as much as possible about what it takes to make and market a film or television program. This is important for a couple of reasons.

First, knowing the filmmaker's challenges may help you make sense of seemingly unrealistic demands. For example, if you know that very often on a television movie, an air date is scheduled before production is even finished, you might better understand why it is important for you to start doing research and thematic development or even start writing cues well before there is a "final cut" (which is sort of a mythological concept anyway).

Secondly, imagine this. A director says to you, "I like the idea of adding four cellos but isn't that going to add to your copying expenses, and will that require a larger and more expensive studio?" Wow. After you peel yourself off the floor, don't you think you'll have more appreciation for this person who actually has an understanding of what you do? Well it works both ways. Few people show empathy for the folks at the top. People are mostly focused on their own little world and the difficulties therein. You might endear yourself to the filmmaker by demonstrating a little understanding for what he is up against.

PEOPLE SCHOOL (SKILLS)

Some clichés are true. None more so than "People like to work with people they like." You may be a brilliant composer, but who needs brilliant? Remember, music appreciation is subjective. We, who have studied music most of our lives, don't always agree on what is either a great score or derivative trash. When people like *you* they want to like your work. They listen *wanting* to like what they hear. If you can't quite believe this then think about the antithesis. What is it like to listen to the work of someone you don't particularly care for? Hard not to find fault, isn't it?

Composers "come on board" a full two-thirds of the way through a project. Our involvement is preceded by *script development, preproduction, production* or *principal photography* and *editing.* To my mind, an established *team personality* exists on each production. While it primarily reflects the personality of the filmmaker, it could also be affected by the director's fight with the producer or the producer's fight with the studio or the firing of two people who sold a bootleg copy of the film on the internet...any number of things of which we are unaware.

We are being adopted into a family that has been through a lot before we even arrive.

Whether you are by nature gregarious or slightly introverted, it is in your best interest to acquire a bit of this team personality. For the extrovert that might mean knowing when to tone down, and for the shy, when to speak out.

It should be mentioned at this point that while everyone on the production team feels comfortable with most aspects of filmmaking, music is probably the one thing that remains the most unsettling. Most film schools don't even mention it, much less compare examples of good and bad scoring.

If the film (now in postproduction) is working well, everyone is a little nervous that you could hurt it. If the film is troubled, they are hoping you can help it. They're anxious either way. Anything you can do to increase their comfort level will be in your best interest.

Now this may sound silly, but if I notice that the director always dresses kind of sharp, I try to wear similar attire. If he or she is always in jeans and a T-shirt, so am I. It's a way of easing concerns about whether we think alike—whether I'll *get* what they have to say or not.

BECOMING AN ASSISTANT

Try to land a position as an assistant to a composer who is working on a project. This is the best kind of advanced education there is: on-the-job training without an extraordinary amount of responsibility. I like to say that this puts you near the fire with no danger of getting burned. Chapter 4 provides suggestions on working with an assistant. This information can just as easily be interpreted for working *as* an assistant. It is exceedingly important that, when you land a position of this kind, your performance be exceptional. Your next step up or down the ladder may depend on how well you do this job.

I receive several resumés and CDs a month. I would never hire anyone to even answer the phone based on a resumé or CD. Even if the resumé is impressive and the music on the CD is wonderful, how am I to know if the person whose name is on the CD is actually responsible for creating it? If he is, how long did it take to write and produce? A year? More? On the other hand, if someone is sitting in my office for a couple of hours, I may feel comfortable enough to give him a cue to write. Face-to-face opportunities are very important.

While working as an assistant, the one sacrilege is trying to persuade the client to use *you* on his next project, rather than the composer for whom you are currently working. However, this business is generational in nature and while your boss is schmoozing the filmmaker you might be creating a relationship with the line producer or the post-production supervisor, and that relationship could prove beneficial in the future. You make a friend of the production assistant this year and next year he's a line producer; five years from now he's executive producer on a major film or television project.

Many levels of education and preparation are necessary to create a successful career in film music. In my experience, once composers start to get work, their studying slows or stops completely. They graduate from students to professionals—at least in their own minds. Therefore, the more time spent learning and gathering information prior to getting that big break, the better.

Bruce Broughton teaches a class on orchestration for the ASCAP Television & Film Scoring Workshop with Richard Bellis.

CHAPTER TWO

PRICING YOUR WORK

Being a film composer is a very expensive hobby.

Film composers, even film composer candidates, are not stupid. It takes a significant degree of intellect to do what we do, however, it seems that the desire to work on a film—much like adolescent sex—outweighs sensibility in many cases. We want to "do it" so badly that we don't care about the repercussions.

"How much do you expect to make per year as a film and television composer?"

That's the way I open my class on Pricing Your Work. The response is almost always the same.

Silence.

If I put this question to a group of pre-med or pre-law students they very likely would be able to come up with a pretty good guesstimate. Maybe the difference is that medical school and law school are expensive. Loans, whether from mom and dad or student/bank loans, have to be justified to the lender. How expensive could it be to become a film composer? After all it's not like if you screw up the score someone will die or go to prison.

Many "would-be" composers to whom I've posed this question have left their homes to move to Los Angeles. Some have even moved their families in order to enroll in a course that could cost upwards of $20,000 for one year. They have purchased new gear and sample libraries and are using their savings to provide for themselves and their families while they study and try to break into the business.

How do they justify the time and expense—and to whom?

Let's take a practical look at the scenario loosely described above.

We'll assume that Jack, working in Chicago, is earning $40,000 a year. Jack is married with no children. His wife is working part-time bringing in around $27,000. The plan is that Jack is going to follow his dream by moving to L.A. and taking a one-year course on film scoring at USC. Jill will go with him because she can probably find work in L.A. They'll try to find a nice apartment for about the same amount they're paying in Chicago, which is around $750 a month or $9,000 a year. The cost of the eight-month program, we'll say, is $24,000.

So, here's what we have:

Jack gives up his income.	-$40,000
Jack pays for the USC course.	-$24,000
Jill picks up only a third of her normal workload because she's new in town.	-$18,000
At $1,200 per month, the apartment they find is actually more expensive than in Chicago.	-$5,400
One year of studying to become a film composer is **costing** Jack and Jill.	-$87,400

Wouldn't you think at least Jill would be interested in what kind of return they're going to see for their investment?

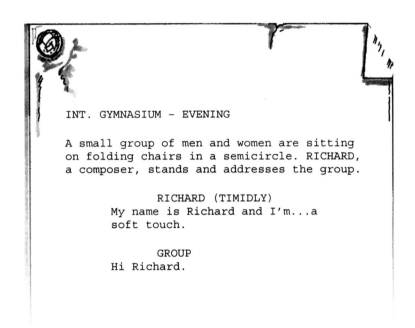

```
INT. GYMNASIUM - EVENING

A small group of men and women are sitting
on folding chairs in a semicircle. RICHARD,
a composer, stands and addresses the group.

                RICHARD (TIMIDLY)
          My name is Richard and I'm...a
          soft touch.

                GROUP
          Hi Richard.
```

Let's face it, film composers are easy.

However, we are not alone in this race to be the softest touch in the industry. Many other people looking to be successful in the entertainment field are vying for the same dubious honor. Emerging actors, directors and editors are all willing to work for little or nothing.

Why do we want to work so badly that we don't care how much it costs us? Two reasons. The one we talk about and the one we don't talk about. First, the one we *don't* talk about.

Because it's fun! It's the movies. Hey, it looks like work to other people but it's really just fun. It looks like work to our spouses who take over all of our responsibilities while we go into our studios and "work." It's a free pass for weeks at a time from getting the car repaired, getting groceries, taking the dog to the groomer, picking up the laundry. Freedom to get up in the morning, make our way to the studio where we join rhythms with melodies and pit soundscaping against French horns. Of course, sooner or later other people start getting involved and telling us what to do, but that's the subject of another chapter.

Okay, now here's the reason we *do* talk about, or at least think about.

We are willing to work for less than we should in order to gain experience, credits and make contacts. Now this one would normally make sense, because since the beginning of craftsmanship there have been apprentices, and this is classic apprenticeship strategy.

THE APPRENTICE SYSTEM

In the 18TH century when folks would go to Paul Revere's shop looking to have a silver tea set made, they might find that Paul himself was either too busy (fighting the British) or too expensive and instead ask for his apprentice to make the set. It would cost less and while they were fully aware of the difference between Paul's smithing skills and the apprentice's, they were okay with it because they were saving a good deal of money (maybe this tea set was for their country house).

The ability to discern the difference between the work of the master and that of the apprentice is one of two very important criteria that must be met in order for the apprentice system to work. The other criteria is the ratio of apprentices to masters. When there is an overabundance of apprentices the economy of that particular craft is threatened. Now you have entry-level people willing to work below market value, competing with other entry-level people also willing to work below market value, and the consumer sees their work as every bit as good as the experienced, master craftsmen's. The result is a new, lower market value. The tragic bottom line is that those who worked hard for less in order to move up the ladder now find that "up the ladder" doesn't pay what it once did.

This is the current state of *our* industry.

So, should you turn down work that pays less than the work is worth? If you do will it affect the economy in a positive way?

No and no. There is a way to, in effect, give it away while doing minimal damage to the industry and to your future.

The subject of film score is sorely neglected in most film schools. Consequently, the emerging filmmaker may not know how music is supposed to *service* the film. This often results in the filmmaker not being able to tell the difference between an excellent score that enhances the film and a mediocre score that merely plays in the background. You can see how this would take its toll on the perceived importance of film music.

This same neglect (by film schools) is responsible for the filmmaker not knowing how to budget for a score, how many people are involved or how many days the composer needs to create and produce that score. Filmmakers need to learn about music in film and their only source of that information may well be the first composer they hire. Maybe you.

There are two primary problems with working for less than the value of the work: precedent and perception. Let's take at look at these.

PRECEDENT AND PERCEPTION

It's the busiest travel day of the year and you have to fly. To help relieve some stress, you decide to hire a limo to take you to the airport. The limo charges you $60 each way. This then becomes the standard in your mind. The next time you use a limo to get to the airport, $60 becomes the price to beat. If you find a limo company that charges $55, that becomes the new standard. This assumes that there is no *perceptible* difference in the service.

A few weeks later you are forced to use a different company that charges you $70 each way. This limo is a newer model and provides fresh pillows, magazines and beverages. A higher price with better service might become your new standard.

If a filmmaker offers you $5,000 for a score and you simply say okay, it becomes that filmmaker's standard. That is what a score now costs and that figure will be in the budget for her next film. You have established a precedent and who knows, her next composer might be...you.

Okay, now for perception, also known as quality/economic typecasting. Take as an example the limo company that charged you $55—the lowest price. In terms of service, it was not as good as the company that charged you $70, was it? You will likely think of them as the "economy class" of limos while you think of the $70 company as "first class." This is perception. If you merely say "yes" to the film with the $5,000 budget, you will be perceived as a $5,000 composer. As that filmmaker starts to work on bigger and better projects it is likely she will use more experienced and higher-priced actors, directors of photography, editors and composers.

What we want is to be perceived as high-end professionals who have decided to do this project for a variety of reasons that warrant a significant reduction in our normal fee. This perception is predicated on actually *having* a normal fee.

If a store is selling an item at a sale price and they don't post the pre-sale price for comparison, how can anyone really appreciate the deal they're getting?

FEES AND HARD COSTS

A score consists of two distinct parts: the *creation* (intelligent design) of the music and the *production* (evolution) of that which you have created. When the entire score is acoustic and everything is played by "live" musicians these two parts are easily distinguishable, but with an electronic or electro-acoustic score the line can get blurred.

Your *fee* is compensation for your creative work, while the production expenses are considered reimbursable *hard costs.* That is, those things and services for which you must pay. The budget then must be broken into these two categories.

Why?

If you need to, you can discount your fee but the hard costs must be covered by the filmmaker or the production company. If you end up paying for the hard costs, you become an investor, otherwise known as a producer. Producers are entitled to have input. No one really wants you to have input, they usually have plenty already.

The fee covers your time, your education, your talent, your studio and equipment or tools. It represents those musical tasks you do *or* would have to pay someone to do if you were not able to perform.

These services are:

Spotting/Creative Meetings/Show and Tell
Music Editing (sometimes on low-budget projects)
Composition
Orchestration/Sequencing
Conducting/Finessing the Electronic Performance
Mixing (supervision at least)
Transferring/Formatting (supervision at least)

In the list above I have equated Orchestration and Sequencing. When you decide what instrument or sound should be playing a certain part, that is orchestration. The method of input, be it notes on paper or notes in a sequence track, is not what the orchestrator gets paid for. Rather, it is the decisions he or she makes that are worth something.

This is also a job that—at one time or another—may have to be done by someone other than yourself, so it is helpful to place a value on it. This is true even though, when scoring electronically, these decisions may seem to be part and parcel of the multitasking composer's work. If you're able to do two jobs at once should you only charge for one? Isn't the person who can do two things concurrently more valuable than a person who can only do one thing at a time? Now this is important: You do not have to charge for each job that you do but you must place a value on each.

I have also equated Conducting and Finessing the Electronic Performance. Once the orchestration is written and on the music stands, the conductor finesses the performance of the orchestra. This period of finessing must also be done to the electronic sequence before you commit to the mix. The process usually consists of adjusting velocities, creating dynamics, crescendos, diminuendos, bowings, sforzandos, etc.

So these things: *Spotting/Creative Meetings, Composition, Orchestration/Sequencing, Conducting/Finessing, Mixing* and *Transferring/Formatting* constitute fees paid to you for your time and talent. If there is something on this list that you must hire someone else to do, that item becomes one of your "hard costs." The hard costs are "must have, must pay for" items such as:

Musicians
Copying
Payroll Service
Tape/Pro Tools or equivalent – Record – Mix – Transfer/Format
Studio Time – Record
Studio Time – Mix
Studio Time – Transfer/Format
Scoring Mixer – Record
Scoring Mixer – Mix
Scoring Mixer – Transfer/Format
Studio Rentals – Record (mics, preamps, etc.)
Studio Rentals – Mix (reverbs)
Studio Rentals – Transfer/Format
Piano Tuning
Instrument Cartage/Rentals
Messenger

The hard costs should be considered **NON-NEGOTIABLE**.

HOW MUCH ARE YOU WORTH?

I find that if I take a look at what other people, both in and outside our industry, are making per hour it helps to put things in perspective.

Here are some examples of hourly wages:

Plumber: $64.50
Plumber's helper: $25.50
Housekeeper: $12–18
Gardener: $20
Attorney: $250–500 and up

Now, let's take a look at the approximate per-hour rate of some of the people with whom we work on a TV movie:

Sideman (single-scale musician): $90 plus fringes
Principal Player: $135–180 plus fringes
Scoring Mixer: $75–250

Next we'll examine how many hours it takes to complete and deliver a score. Before we do however, let me remind you that when you are doing a score for less than market value, it is even more important that the score be extremely well done. If you work too fast or without enough budget to produce the score properly, you will merely hurt your reputation—for no money. This is a lose-lose situation.

When we start to examine how long it takes to do the job we should be thinking of the worst-case scenario. Your spouse has the flu, the dog has diarrhea, you've got a headache and the housekeeper is on vacation. The car only starts intermittently and your parents are coming in from the Midwest for a visit.

Now, how many minutes of music can you write per day?

The standard answer, since the days when I started writing, has always been three minutes a day. Most days that would mean at least 10 working hours. If you're smart, you will be thinking about two minutes a day instead. Remember, this must be a great score in order to make the exercise worthwhile.

So, let's take that $5000 music budget for example.

If it's three minutes a day for a 50 minute score, you would need 17 working days to complete the writing. If your days are indeed 10 hours then you would be putting in 170 hours on the creation of the score.

This doesn't include being the music editor, the orchestrator or the conductor, it is merely the composer's hours. Now pick an hourly wage from the list at left. Maybe the scoring mixer; more than the plumber but less than the concertmaster. This is just a number to start with. I know how much you want to be able to justify taking the job, and you're afraid that if you pick a high hourly wage it will scare off the filmmaker. That's all right. Fortitude comes with experience. Most often a bad experience.

All right, $75 per hour x 170 hours is $12,750 worth of composition. My god! That's more than two and a half times the whole music budget!!!

Yes.

So who's wrong? Are you asking too much for your time, talent, studio and gear or is there a problem with the budget? After all, they've done many of these movies, they must know what the music is worth.

Well, let's take a look at an alternative scenario. Let's say you value your work at the housekeeper rate of about $15 per hour, 170 hours x $15 per hour is $2,550. Now, that's more like it. You now have $2,450 to spend on production hard costs. Never mind that the housekeeper's tools cost about $300 and will last for two or three years while your tools cost around $30,000 and will last about 18 months. The housekeeper also works 40 hours per week and probably 46 weeks per year for a total of 1840 hours. If you average 170 hours per film as in our example, you would have to land almost 11 films every year to equal the housekeeper's annual gross income. That's gross—as in before taxes.

Shopping List
1 writer
1 director
2 asst. directors
3 lead actors
2 days w/ helicopter
36 supporting cast members
1 location manager
1 day crane w/ operator
1 casting director
1 composer

Producers know how to shop. Part of their job is knowing what things cost. If you are going to negotiate with a producer for more money and you can actually get past the "No" stage, you will have a much better chance of getting what you need if you can break down the costs. The other benefit to having a cost breakdown is fortitude. Your fortitude. When you find yourself negotiating with someone who has far more negotiating experience than you, having the courage of your convictions is of great benefit. If you've done the numbers and know you're right, you may actually emerge from a negotiation unscathed and maybe even victorious.

If the director needs an extra day of filming at a certain location, the director and location manager may have to justify the need and present to the producer exactly what the costs will be for that one additional day of hotel for cast and crew, security at the set, catering, transportation, etc.

Composers may never be called upon to present the breakdown of costs but should have it and know the cost of everything. The tighter the budget, the more you need the breakdown.

The Proposal

So here is the hypothetical offer you've just received:

You are being asked to score a movie that is 96 minutes long. No one knows exactly how much music is needed but the filmmakers suspect it to be primarily electronic with some orchestral sections. Their music budget is $35,000.

Do you take it? Can you do it for this price?

If you just say yes at this point it would be like calling a house painter on the phone and asking if he could paint your house for $700. No dimensions, just could he do it? Wouldn't you be a bit suspicious if he said yes?

You must at this point break down the costs. But you have important unknowns and consequently your only choice is to plug temporary values into the equation. So we start with an "if-then" statement:

If there are 45 minutes of music in this film and if 12 min-utes are orchestral, then 33 minutes will be electronic. We can use this as a contingency later if we find that there are significantly more minutes of music than originally thought and we must renegotiate.

Deliverables

We will also have to assume the deliverable requirements. It was not too many years ago that the deliverable format was always magnetic striped film. The only variable was how many tracks. Today there are a number of formats in which you may be required to deliver. They can signifi-cantly affect your overall budget and so I suggest you start here. This would be one of the first questions to ask when preparing to create a budget. If no one knows or seems to care then you may have the opportunity of making this decision yourself, although at some point down the road there's a good chance that someone will jump out of the shadows caring very much and give you the actual require-ments. Chances are you will be at the wrong sample rate or version of Pro Tools or something. The person to ask is the post-production supervisor and it might not be a bad idea to double-check with the dubbing stage.

Let's assume that you are going to record and deliver on Pro Tools with the appropriate sample and frame rates. You'll need a studio with a good sized live room for the orchestra session, and you'll mix electronics and orchestral cues in a smaller studio to save money.

Okay, now we are ready to start figuring. Please keep in mind that this is only an example. You may need more or less of the items listed. For instance, I have not listed a score reader or a conductor.

Hard Costs

➤ **PRO TOOLS**
Pro Tools Rental for recording,
mixing and preparing deliverables
4 days @ 400 per day   **$1600**

Pro Tools operator for recording session
(We'll assume that the scoring mixer
will run Pro Tools for the mix and
creating deliverables)   **$1300**

➤ **STUDIO**
12 minutes of orchestra =
3 hours of studio time @ $300 per hour
(In my experience recording 4 minutes
per hour with an orchestra is SCREAMIN')   **$900**

Studio setup = 3 hours @ $150 per hour   **$450**
Studio tear down = 1 hour @ $150   **$150**

Piano tuning   **$75**
(Most L.A. studios insist on doing this
whether you want it or not)

Mix studio for 45 minutes of music =
2 (10-hour) days @ $1000 per day   **$2,000**

➤ **SCORING MIXER**
Engineer (scoring mixer):
orchestral recording = 6 hours @ $75
*(Includes 3 hours of setup time
before the session)*   **$450**

Engineer (scoring mixer):
mix = 20 hours @ $75   **$1,500**

➤ **RENTALS**
Lexicon reverb rental:
mix = 2 days @ $150 per day   **$300**

➤ **COPYING**
Copying for orchestral cues =
12 minutes @ $250 per minute   **$3,000**
*(This has to be an estimate based
on number of minutes of music.
Remember: if the minutes of music
increase significantly, so will this number.)*

GRAND TOTAL OF HARD COSTS   **$11,725**

Music budget of $35,000
minus $11,725 =   **$23,275 left to spend**

The Orchestra

Next we'll look at the number of players in the orchestra. While the orchestra is considered a "hard cost," it obviously can be a variable one, so you'll need some kind of per-player price in order to easily try different combinations of numbers. A player is different from a unit (one single-scale player) because the player might require a double, double-scale or some other form of premium payment. The per-player figure that you use should be an average cost that takes into account fringes for all and premium payments for some of the players. For the sake of this example we'll use $325 per player per three-hour session.

You'll want, let's say, eighteen vlns, six vlas, four vlcs, one bass, four w.w.s, one horn, two perc., one keyboard, one harp, one contractor.

Total people 39 @ $325 = **$12,675**
Cartage for harp, perc, bass and vlcs will be around **$750**

TOTAL ORCHESTRA COST: $13,425

$23,275 "Left to Spend"
minus Orchestra Costs of $13,425 = **$9,850 left for your fee**

Okay, now we have figured the *Non-Negotiable* costs. Let's move on to:

Fees

For each of the jobs we as composers do, we have to determine a common form of measurement in order to value it. While not always easy, nor absolutely perfect, the easiest common measurement is per hour.

How many minutes worth of each task can you do per hour? These answers should be based on the aforementioned "worst-case" scenario.

➤ **SPOTTING** a 96-minute film = **8 hours**

➤ **COMPOSITION** - 3 minutes per (10-hour) day
45 minutes of music divided by 3 (minutes per day) =
15 (10-hour) days or **150 hours**

➤ **ORCHESTRATION/ACOUSTIC AND ELECTRONIC**

We have to get a little creative. A professional orchestrator will average two to four "score pages" per hour. A "score page" is defined as four measures. Find a tempo that you think might represent an average of all the cues. Then use this formula:

Average tempo mm =   80 beats per minute
                    x   45 mins (of score)
                    = 3600 beats
OR

                     900 4/4 bars
                   ÷   4 (bars to the "score page")
                   = 225 "score pages"

225 pages divided by 4 pages per hour = 56.25 hours.
Say **56 hours.**

➤ **CONDUCTING/FINESSING**
Conducting (orchestral session): 3 hours
Finessing: 10 hours
Total: 13 hours

➤ **MIX SUPERVISION** 2 (10-hour) days = **20 hours**

GRAND TOTAL OF HOURS IN FEE CATEGORY = 247 HOURS

Once again, pick an hourly rate that you want to start with, for instance $60 per hour. (Way too low for what we do but for the sake of a "craftsman's wage," i.e., lead carpenter, plumber, etc., let's start here.)

$60 per hour x 247 hours = **$14,820**

The Moment of Truth

So now we total up:

$14,820 fee (@ $60 per hour)
$13,425 orchestra
$11,725 hard costs

———————————————————

Total is $39,970
which means you're ***over budget by $4,970.***

Now we must examine all the possibilities available to us.

The first is to assume that the amount of the budget is too low and prepare a case for getting an increase. The breakdown you've just created should be a very good tool for your presentation.

The second choice still puts the ball in the filmmaker's court. We propose the possibility that an acoustic orchestra might not be affordable and can we talk about either emulation or a smaller ensemble. After all, by cutting out the orchestra you also cut out the need for a studio with a large live room, a scoring mixer for that day and copying—not to mention piano tuning.

The third possibility is to reduce the size of the orchestra. This might mean you can record in a smaller, less expensive studio as well as diminish the cost of copying.

Finally, when all other options have been exhausted, you begin to negotiate your fees away. While it should not be necessary to break down your fees for the filmmaker you may find it convincing to tell them the hourly wage that you will have to settle for.

If you subtract your over-budget figure ($4,970) from your calculated fee of $14,820 (figured at $60 per hour) you get $9,850, or $39.88 per hour. Since this amount represents an hourly wage less than any of the players in the orchestra, the scoring mixer and even the piano tuner, let's take a look at what you might ask from the project in exchange for your financial sacrifice.

THE POINTS OF NEGOTIATION

1.) **Full revenue stream from the public performance of the music** (writer's and publisher's share). You might license the entire score, retaining ownership of the copyright. Any production company attorney will complain that if you own the copyright that will tie the hands of the company when it comes to marketing the film. In actuality, you can issue the company a license in perpetuity for the galaxy and still retain ownership of the copyright. This will give the company the right to sell or distribute its film with your music, without consulting you. You don't think the company owns the copyright to that Beatle's song it used, do you? Just make sure that the right to use the music is only within the context of that particular film. You don't want people creating their own music library of your cues.

2.) All rights to produce and sell a CD and to use artwork from the film on the sleeve.

3.) Box-office (or secondary market) "bumps." These are payments to you when certain predetermined financial or market targets for the film are met. For example, when the film reaches recoupment or when the DVD distribution deal is made then there will be an additional payment. It is sometimes a good way to say, "I'll help you now but when you make more money, then I would like to be fully compensated." In other words, you become a team player.

4.) More time to write. Fast is expensive. You may have to bring in help on a tight schedule, which adds to your hard costs.

5.) A multiple picture deal.

6.) Inclusion in the official entourage that accompanies the film to festivals. With expenses.

Now, let's say you settle for the $9,850 ($39.88 per hour) for your fee. And let's further assume that you are very successful at this low-budget film category and, with your many connections, are able to land five films a year. If you average the same 247 hours on each film, that will mean that your annual *gross* would be $49,250 per year. After taxes that might be a net of $35,952.50. That's just over $2,900 a month. Can you (and your family) live on that? Can you live on that and buy new gear and upgrades that you will need to stay in business? And more importantly,

Can you get five films a year?

Okay, let's assume you can get five films a year. In order to get that many films you would most likely have to take up full-time residence in L.A. So, what's that cost?

COST OF ~~LIVING~~ *SURVIVING* AND WORKING IN L.A.

(per month)

Rent *(one-bedroom apartment that allows you to play/create music)*	$1000
Utilities *(gas, electric, water – air conditioning in summer while working)*	$150
Telephone *(including cell/Internet)*	$125
Car *(modest newer car payment)*	$250
Auto Insurance *(minimal)*	$100
Gas *(for car)*	$100
Food *(based on $10 per day)*	$300
Health Insurance *(no dependents)*	$150
Instrument/Studio Insurance	$50
Promotion *(lunches, dinners, events, photos, blank media, printing, postage, supplies)*	$80
Studio expenses *(new gear, software, CDs, cables, maintenance)*	$200
Clothing Allowance *(purchase, cleaning, laundry)*	$150
TOTAL MINIMAL MONTHLY EXPENSES	$2,655
	$31,860 per year

BOTTOM LINE

The bottom line is that you cannot work for very long in the low end of the marketplace. Unless you prefer a spartan lifestyle, you must move up. Writing well and hoping to be discovered is simply not enough. Everyone writes well. Well, almost everyone.

The Back End

As we come to the end of this chapter it seems only fitting that I mention "the back end." The source of my annual "nut" for a number of years has been the money I receive from my Performing Rights Organization (PRO). With "front end" money at an all-time low, more and more composers have become aware of the importance of the royalties paid through the PROs. There is sometimes a tendency to marginalize the importance of these royalties when the number of projects you've done is low. It's true that if you have primarily been doing theatrical films as opposed to television you might be totally unimpressed with your royalties; that's because theatrical films shown in the USA don't pay royalties until they are shown on television. On the other hand, if you've done any television work, you are not only aware of this revenue stream but can get pretty excited projecting its potential as your career grows. Never, ever, ever sign away your "writer's share" of these royalties. That single act could begin to erode this revenue stream for all film and television composers.

I would like to put a couple of misconceptions to bed.

I still hear from emerging composers that they are afraid if they bring up the subject of royalties, the filmmaker or production company will balk at the potential fiduciary responsibility.

There is absolutely no cost, present or future, to the filmmaker or production company for performing rights royalties.

This money, collected and distributed by the likes of ASCAP, BMI and SESAC in the United States, SOCAN in Canada and other PROs in the rest of the world, comes from the exhibitors (broadcasters, venues, etc.) not the production company. An example of how the system works might be that NBC, ABC and CBS each pay annual license fees to ASCAP, BMI and SESAC, entitling them to use any and all music represented by those organizations. The PROs then are responsible for figuring out (via cue sheets) who wrote the music on each of the shows broadcast by each network and distribute, from the license fee collected, the appropriate amount to each composer or songwriter.

The second misconception is that if you want to write for features, stay away from television.

My friends, if I haven't made my point by now let me state one final time:

This is a buyer's market.

You cannot manipulate your career in a buyer's market. It will take you where it will. You are just along for the ride.

There are people who swear that they started getting feature work as soon as they started turning down television work. These, most often, are people who were working on a hot television show that got them recognized. Had they turned down *that* show because they wanted to be "feature composers" they never would have garnered the notice of feature filmmakers. Your career is not yours to manipulate. You may do some mid-course alterations once you have been noticed, but to start your career voyage sitting on the dock, waiting for the *right* ship to come in, is folly.

Take all good work.

So, how do you decide which projects represent *good* work? Which ones represent the film projects that will take you up the ladder fastest?

I believe there are five possible reasons to take a job:
1.) To make *good* money
2.) To get a *good* credit
3.) To foster a *good* relationship
4.) To have a *wonderful* experience
5.) To get a *good* recording of something you don't already have on your demo "reel"

If you can get any three out of the five, take it. If you can get two out of five and there is no other work on the horizon, take it. But, notice carefully the italicized words. It must be a good credit, a good relationship and so on.

Getting these things may be dependent on having adequate time and a workable budget. Doing someone a favor by working too fast, without a decent budget, and producing a mediocre score will not foster a good relationship. Nor will it create a good credit or a good demo.

Give yourself a predetermined number of projects on which you will make less than what you know you should. In my humble opinion anyone writing original music for less than $150 per hour better be getting something else of equal value in return.

Finally, here is the age-old triangle theory that will help to explain to clients the options they have. You may have any two of the three things listed.

"You may have it _____ and _____ but it won't be _____."

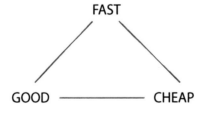

CHAPTER THREE

GETTING WORK

You can be a composer anywhere at any time:
in the shower, in the car, anywhere.
However, you are only a film composer
when you have a film to work on.
Getting work is essential to
actually being what you call yourself.

For those of you who turned immediately to this chapter, I regret that there is no definitive answer to the question: "How do I find work?" Ideas and strategies, yes. Definitive answers, no. It would be wonderful if the quality of your music was the deciding factor in whether or not you worked in this industry but alas, that is not the case.

DOES QUALITY COUNT?

It is important that you hone your writing skills to the highest level achievable. Will anybody notice? Will you receive compliments on the French horn voicings or acknowledgement of how the harp part is reminiscent of Ravel? Not likely. But a high level of quality will give you a high level of self-confidence, and self-confidence can make an impression with musical and nonmusical people alike. If you feel good about your abilities, that feeling will communicate to those with whom you are meeting.

Is confidence enough to get you work? No.

No one thing is enough to get you work. Well, maybe blood. Nepotism will give you a leg up, but only briefly unless you really have the goods. Even relatives are in this business to be successful and if Uncle Jack, the producer, perceives that your music is responsible for "bringing down" his film or television show, it doesn't matter whose child you are or to whom you're married. "Next!"

In order to understand why the hiring practices are so unpredictable, we must examine several circumstances that prevail in this industry.

Recently, I had the opportunity to speak with three young filmmakers. Each had graduated from a Southern California film school about two years prior to our meeting.

The conversation started with their questions to me: "How much time does a composer need to create the score for a film?" and, "When should I hire the composer…when I hire the rest of the crew?"

Each of these young directors had attended a different film school: The University of Southern California, Loyola Marymount and Cal State, Northridge. I answered their questions and then asked them, "How much of your curriculum was dedicated to the musical score?" They were unanimous. None. No mention of music as part of the filmmaking process. Needless to say I was stunned. To a significant extent, this educational void is the reason some filmmakers cannot "cast" a composer based on the quality of his work. If a filmmaker has never been introduced to an A/B comparison of a scene well-scored versus one in which the music does nothing, how are they supposed to know what well-crafted music can do for their film…what music is *supposed* to do for their film? The first person they learn from is the first composer they work with, and for a student or entry-level director, that composer may or may not be the best teacher.

Okay, so **Factor #1** is that those people responsible for hiring us often are not trained to adjudicate our work. This is a very big deal. It begs the question: *What are they adjudicating?* Age, gender, ethnicity, energy? I actually had an experience that gave me a glimpse of this scenario.

I was interviewing two architects. I love architecture but know very little about how it does what it does. The first of the two drove up to my house in his Porsche. Showed me pictures of houses he'd done, far more expensive than mine. My mind was already made up by the time he left that he was too expensive both in fee and in concept, even though we never talked about money.

I went to the office of the second architect, which was stylish and pristine, as you might expect, but was also modest in size. More importantly, this architect somewhat resembled my older brother in looks and mannerisms, so he got the job. In the end, he did great work, so was my decision-making process justified? Not at all!

There are just times when we get to be President of the F---ing Lucky Club. This was one of those times.

Factor #2 is that music is serving a much more sophisticated and subtle purpose today than ever before. This makes Factor #1 all the more dramatic. Let's examine this a bit further.

WHAT IS MUSIC SUPPOSED TO DO?

The earliest use of music with film was a piano player in the same room with the audience and the projector. The purpose of the music was to cover/distract from the noise of the projector. This "film music" was practical and easy to direct: "Keep playing!"

Progress moved the projector into its own booth. Silent movies were still the thing and the piano player, or sometimes a small pit orchestra, was now charged with giving inflection to the "dialogue" written on the screen. With "talkies" came sound, however, there was still a great need for all the things that were missing. Music provided, among other things, the color and the vista or scope that was impossible to achieve with B&W film and a limited array of lenses and photographic techniques. Enter Technicolor and CinemaScope, and music's duties changed again. We let go of color, loosened our grip on scope and focused on the other things that could not be shown on the screen. We were sex, violence, magic, special FX.

Fast forward to today. Everything is on the screen. Special FX have never been cooler, sex sells, and language and violence have a large fan club.

So what is music doing these days in the process of filmmaking? Why is it still an integral part of each new film? It is probably the most overtly artificial ingredient in all but the most fictional films or animation. I say *overtly* because many if not all aspects of filmmaking are essentially artificial. The best way to explain this is with a famous story involving the Alfred Hitchcock film, *Lifeboat.*

Hugo Friedhofer had been hired to do the score but Hitchcock had refused to have score playing during any of the scenes in the lifeboat (most of the movie). Legendary composer David Raksin confronted Hitchcock one day on the studio lot and asked, "How come no music?" Hitchcock replied, "Out in the middle of the ocean, where's the orchestra?" Quick-witted Raksin fired back: "Out in the middle of the ocean, where's the camera?"

The darkened room in which we view a movie is the first artificial aspect of filmmaking, followed by editing, multiple camera angles, focused hearing (focused on the dialogue), stunts and all the rest. But the truth of the matter is that in "real life" our brain actually does some of these filmic things. When looking at someone we do "crop" out much of the periphery. We do adjust our hearing in order to filter out extraneous noises. Only occasionally, however, do we score our lives with music played in our brain. Childhood games with the traditional chase cue: *nun-nun-nun-nun-nun-nun-nun-nun-naaaaah* are one of very few instances—at least for me.

So, what *does* music do in films today?

What? You expect me to give you an answer in writing, only to be proven wrong or, worse, outdated over time. No way. This is for you to think about. Think seriously about it because the purpose of today's film music is more vague and subjective than ever before. Reason enough to make the study of film music mandatory for young filmmakers. Formulate an opinion and a response to the question, should it ever be asked of you. And, just as a tip, try to stay away from the esoteric "It's the heart and soul of the film." Writers and directors may have a slightly different view.

Factor #3 has to do with how many new film and television composers are joining the community every year.

At one time there were so few film composers that filmmakers found it necessary to overlook some of their personal preferences when deciding with whom they would work. Personality flaws, conflicting ideologies often had to be set aside in order to hire the right composer. By contrast, today's filmmakers can almost dictate the race, religion, gender and height of the composer they want to score their film.

Over the past 15 years, for any number of possible reasons, interest in writing music for film, television and other media has exploded. The popularity of John Williams' *Star Wars* score, the availability of electronics and sample libraries, an unfortunately diminished audience of concertgoers, the ease with which you can access entertainment media in your home, all may play a part in this overwhelming interest in our craft.

When there appears to be a popular interest in any given subject, colleges and universities—constantly competing for their share of the higher education dollars—develop courses in that subject. A certain amount of promotion follows to ensure that the time and expense devoted to establishing that new curriculum is justified and amortized. The result is that we have more young people graduating from college wanting to follow the career path of media music. The hypothetical projection is that degrees will be offered (some are currently being offered) and those degree holders will become the teachers of even more media music courses. This system will, if it hasn't already, produce way more composers than are required for the available work.

Few occupations in the entertainment business are as singular as ours. That is to say, whether the film is an epic, utilizing great numbers of actors, crew members, animators, stunt personnel, teamsters, etc., or a small ensemble cast in a courtroom setting and requiring a minimal crew, there will only be one composer and one director. There may be multiple writers, sound FX editors, even film editors, but only a single composer.

THE COMPOSER'S AGENT

So, maybe you need an agent.
"But are agents really interested in our careers?" you ask.
Some are—sometimes.

Look, agents have mortgages, property taxes, kids going to college, divorces and all the rest. They need to make a living. A good living. Years ago when the front-end money—that which agents commission—started to diminish, composers working out of their home studios found it relatively easy to absorb the reduction in revenue. Agents, on the other hand, don't work out of their homes. They have real overhead. Office rental, staff, phones, computers, subscriptions to production reference services. Real, cost-of-doing-business expenses.

They take a commission on the front end. The percentage depends on whether it's a fee or package deal and on how much of a "cash cow" a particular composer client is. When a studio calls looking for a composer, it is not good business to let that studio or filmmaker go elsewhere (to another agency). Therefore, an agent's efforts are sometimes limited by how much resistance is encountered when trying to sell a particular client to a filmmaker or studio.

"Don't call us, we'll call you" was a phrase that I grew up hearing as a child actor in the 50s. It is the current mantra of the composer's agent, whose client list—"stable" if you will—has to be populated by *working* composers. If you don't have an agent but happen to make it onto a "short list" for a series, let's say, you will in all likelihood hear from a number of agents. You will have offers of more lunches than you can handle.

Generally, agents can't afford to spend a great deal of time on non-revenue producing tasks. Building a career for a certain young composer would fall under that heading. Career building has been taken over by people who receive a fee regardless of whether your career blossoms or not.

THE RANDOM CARD

Random is a double-edged sword. When you are an emerging film composer it is a blessing. It means that with little or no experience and few if any credits, there is a chance that you could land a hit series any day now. As you professionally mature, accumulate credits and maybe garner a few nominations and one or two awards, the random card becomes extremely unsettling. You have, over the years, acquired a nice home with a mortgage, nice car, nice kids, nice gardener, housekeeper, etc., all needing their share of your revenue stream, or revenue trickle as is sometimes the case. The fact that your experience, credits and time served don't count for as much as you think they should can be downright disheartening.

During the last class of the semester I was giving my students the usual "Don't be impatient. It will take time, maybe three or four years to start getting *regular* work." Within eight months, one of those students landed a series that became very successful and led to another series that led to a pretty decent film, and another and another. You just never know.

Another example of the random card involves a student who, while driving in Beverly Hills, was rear-ended by a very nice car. The driver of that car was insistent that he didn't want this to go through his insurance company. The composer student was nice about it and the relieved driver turned out to be a producer who was shooting a film at the time. Guess who did the music?

The random card works both ways. For instance, it's very possible that the producer who rear-ended the student had a director who had promised a friend of hers that since she was directing this film she would almost certainly be able to get her friend in as the composer. An *almost* sure thing.

You might think of this business as a parallel to professional gambling. Just because you know everything there is to know about how to play the game, you are not guaranteed a winning hand. And, that person sitting on your left at the blackjack table, who just split 10s, may very well end up being dealt two aces.

So how do we, and the professional gambler, tip the odds in our favor? The professional gambler plays a lot. Much more than the tourist. Every day perhaps. We too must be out there in places where the random card can manifest. Unless your plumber has a sister who's working on a movie that is in desperate need of a composer, you're going to have to leave your house. Often. Join the Society of Composers &

Lyricists if you are in the Southern California or New York areas, or the Guild of Canadian Film Composers. Go to all the screenings and seminars, strike up conversations, let other composers know what your strengths are.

Agents subscribe to production reference services. You can too. These services, primarily set up to benefit actors and others involved in production, send out lists of film and television projects that are either in development, preproduction or production. These lists include the studio or production company and the contact information. In addition, they might list the names of actors who have committed to the project and often a brief description of the subject matter. Select those projects that you actually have a chance of landing. If Tom Cruise is listed in the cast, it's unlikely that the producers will be interested in an emerging composer. As a matter of fact, they most likely will be given a list of acceptable composers who are of a certain stature. They must choose from this list or fight a long, uphill battle to get someone they consider a talented unknown into a high-profile film.

Meet, submit, write, record and demo constantly. The way to hedge the odds against the random selection process is with the shotgun approach.

Be everywhere. Have everything. (Business cards, CDs, DVDs, discreetly out of sight of course.)

If you live in a country that has a less active film and television industry than the U.S. and Canada, it might be wise to stay there for a while. Try to find and meet the premier filmmaker(s) in that country. You'll likely be competing with fewer film composers, and creating a name and reputation at home may give you an edge when and if you do decide to move elsewhere.

I have found over the years that good fortune comes from the most unexpected sources and at the most unexpected times. Cultivate the unexpected.

Put another way...

When you realize that everything good comes "out of left field," your job is to go to the ballpark every day.

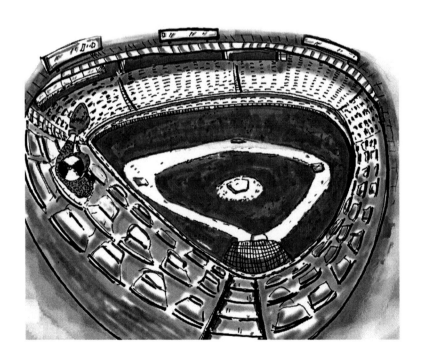

CHAPTER FOUR

SPOTTING

Producer: *"Now, this is the most important cue and I want you to write two versions."*
Composer: *"Really?"*
Producer: *"Yes, the first version the way you think it should be scored and the second version…well…different."*

Okay, it can get weird from time to time, but the spotting session is one of my favorite parts of the process. It is the time when the composer is seen in the *best possible* light. You are "the chosen one." Out of all the submissions, all the demos, all the political pullings and pushings, you have emerged the winner! You haven't had a chance to screw up anything yet and everyone is happy to meet you—well, almost everyone—and they want to let you know that they are looking forward to all that you are going to add to this film or television project of theirs. If I could be a professional spotting guy, take the check and go home it would be a beautiful world. Even the dialogue that's quoted at the beginning of this chapter wouldn't bother me.

If I were to merely describe what the spotting session is supposed to accomplish it would not warrant a chapter. It wouldn't even warrant a paragraph: The purpose of the spotting session is to pick where the music will go and what kind of music it will be. Simple.

The fact that it also represents one of two possible occasions on which you will be spending six to eight hours sitting alongside the director and/or the producer in itself makes it worth exploring in some depth. Let's start by taking a look around the room to see who's in attendance.

THE "USUAL SUSPECTS"

The Director: The visionary head of the project. This is the person who should be your primary guide and partner in scoring the film.

The Producer (Executive): Sometimes creatively involved, sometimes not. Often in television postproduction, the producer will take over from the director who has moved on to another project.

The Film Editor: The editor has more clout than you might imagine. She, after all, has served the wishes of the director (the visionary head) since the first *dailies* started coming in.

She has been involved in all discussions and has made all the changes resulting from those discussions.

Let's take a moment to review the stages of editing that this film has gone through to get to its current state:

> Once principal photography has provided enough footage, the editor begins to assemble the footage following the script. She will continue throughout the entire shooting schedule until the film is complete and significantly over-length.

> When production wraps and the director is available, he and the editor start to create "The Director's Cut." This is not only tradition, it is actually part of the director's contract. He will have a specified number of weeks in which to create his film.

> This version of the film now goes either to the producer or the studio or to a test audience and is subjected to further edits until all the "powers that be" have signed off on it.

The editor has been with the filmmaker through all of these stages. She was there when things were tried and did or didn't work. She is the last person to have (creatively) touched this film. She is also capable, if anyone is, of altering the film to help your work.

If the budget doesn't allow for a music editor to be brought in during production, then the film editor is most likely the person responsible for the temp music you are listening to.

I have had moments of high anxiety while listening to the temp and thinking, *"Is this what they really want?"* only to talk with the film editor who tells me, "We couldn't find anything. I know this isn't right but I needed something to cut to." You can get a great deal of insight from the film editor.

The Music Editor: The music editor is your closest ally. The extent of his participation depends somewhat on the budget of the project. He may have been brought in to temp the film well before you were even hired, or he might be meeting everybody for the first time. Because he will be servicing the music during several stages of writing, recording and dubbing, here I'll only address what he will be doing at the spotting session.

The music editor will be making note of all music starts and stops. He will record any specific ideas that are mentioned concerning the style of music and will confirm delivery requirements including sample and frame rates. He will also coordinate the acquisition and placement of licensed music or songs. Often, by the end of the spotting session the music editor will be able to give the composer a rough idea of how many minutes of original music the composer will be required to write. This is particularly handy in case it turns out to be a much higher number than anyone has anticipated. If that's the case, it gives you the opportunity to at least open the discussion of how this might impact the schedule and the budget.

Music editors work on many more films per year than any single composer and therefore can be a wealth of information.

Music Editor Michael Ryan of Mad 4 Music at his workstation.

Associate Producer and Others: The amount of input you can expect from this group will vary widely. You will have to feel out everyone in the room to find out where the power, wisdom, etc., lies. Most of my spotting sessions have been two-person (composer-director) discussions with limited gallery involvement; however, there have been occasions when they've been five or six person sessions from beginning to end.

THE STUFF

Now let's talk about the stuff, the equipment that might be used in the spotting session. Over the years I have spotted in a screening room, on a Movieola, a Kem, the Avid and on a plain ol' television set. The truth of the matter is that in the 21st century, frame-accurate timings are not that crucial at this juncture. It is expected that you will do some reassessment when you actually start to write the cues.

In the days of our predecessors, there was no way to take the picture back to their writing desk. They had to rely upon the *breakdowns* provided by the music editor. If they needed to see the picture they would arrange for a screening room, a (union) projectionist and delivery of all the reels that were needed. With frame-accurate digitized picture right at our fingertips, we can finesse entrances and exits almost at will. However, anything more than just finessing should be run by the filmmaker. This brings up a point that justifies a slight digression.

It is very easy to become so absorbed in our writing that we lose sight of the fact that the director and/or producer may have things to do other than sit by the phone and wait for our questions or suggestions. Believe me, there is plenty to keep them busy during postproduction so be wise with your phone calls and e-mails. Collect and organize your questions and thoughts. When communicating about a certain scene, use a frame of reference that they can easily decipher to explain where and what your question is. A SMPTE code reference or a scene number or an act number followed by a description of the scene. Something so that they don't have to go through the movie looking for the place you're asking about. If you need to speak with them personally, try sending an e-mail asking what time they might be available to speak with you for about 15 minutes.

Okay, back to the stuff.

I always felt that the Kem, while noisy due to the fact that 35 mm film is running through multiple heads, was a composer-friendly device because its controls were simple and could be run by the director. There was just enough room for two people to sit at the Kem, which created a kind of exclusionary pod for the director and composer.

The latest and fastest form of editing, the digital workstation such as the Avid, provides a spotting session that moves quickly and efficiently. The video and audio have been digitized so as to eliminate "fast forward" and "rewind." The film editor or her assistant will almost always run the Avid.

My *modus operandi* includes a small digital recorder held in my lap and running continuously. I haven't met a director yet who objected to this but there certainly exists the possibility that one could. No matter how sure I am at the spotting session that I will never forget even one word of what's being said—I know better. I have this recording transcribed, paraphrased and categorized by cue number and general comments. In about three or four weeks, with the deadline looming and anxiety growing, when the idea hits me like a bolt out of the blue: "What you need here is a clarinet solo," I will be able to read about how the director's sister used to play clarinet when they were little and how she would hit him on the head with the bell when he wasn't looking. He hates clarinet!

If there has been some political tension within the production and if everyone cannot or will not be present at the spotting session, I have these transcriptions sent around to the "powers that be" so that any differences can be worked out before I start writing. I have never had to use these recordings to prove that "yes, you did say that!" but I guess they might come in handy for that as well.

Now, we've talked about everything and everyone in the room except for...

YOU

Your behavior at the spotting session and each subsequent meeting can signal to filmmakers your experience or inexperience. This then has the potential to either increase their confidence or add to any trepidation or insecurity they might be feeling.

Appreciation of music is highly subjective—personal, if you will. What we think about a piece of music is subject to our likes and dislikes, which have been influenced by the likes and dislikes of our parents, older siblings, friends, mentors and spouse(s). In addition to these personal influences, other things can affect how we feel about a piece of music. Distractions for example. You're listening while in bad traffic and someone cuts you off or you're looking for a street name or an address and you have to turn off the music because you just can't concentrate with "that" playing. Think of the difference when listening to music on vacation as opposed to when you have to leave your house for an appointment in 10 minutes.

Having your cues adjudicated by someone who is concerned about your inexperience is not the optimum audition scenario. Yes, we want to be liked, we want to be funny and charming, but above all we want to be thought of as professional—competent—capable. Here are a few things you can do to foster that image:

Preview the Film

You will be given a copy of the film to preview before the spotting session. Before you watch it, try to recall all that you have been told about the project. People may have told you what they were trying to "say" with the film for example. Maybe they mentioned the demographic audience they were going after. You are about to make your biggest, non-musical contribution to this project. You have something at this moment that no one else involved with the production has. OBJECTIVITY! After you've watched the film once it will never be the same.

This is a very important step.

In a way, it's like a test. For you and for the film. You might be asked if you "got" this or "caught" that or if you "understood the line of dialogue where she says…" The places where you didn't may very well be the places you are most needed *or* need to be particularly careful.

Collect Words and Phrases

Start to assemble non-musical descriptions of the film in general and scenes in particular. It is too early to formulate any specific musical ideas. Wait for some input from the filmmaker. Assess how you think the temp music works and whether or not it is even applicable given the budget.

Just hold off on the three banjos idea until after you meet with the filmmaker.

Make a List

Write down all thoughts and questions. This will save time in spotting, save phone calls later on and maybe score some points for you based on organization. If your thoughts are written down, not only will you remember everything you wanted to say or ask, you can edit or bring up certain things at the most opportune moments.

Try to stay away from phrases like "*I can make this work*" or "*I think I can help this scene.*" The director may be reticent to have you "fix" a film in which she does not perceive a problem. Rather phrases like *"I'd love to be in here"* or *"I'd really like to be a part of this"* may get a warmer reception.

STARTING OFF THE SPOTTING SESSION

This is usually the time for a general discussion about the film and the music. You might get questions about what your first impressions were. You will most likely hear about the director's likes and dislikes as well as her thoughts on specific cues, instruments, etc. The directors I've worked with have definite ideas about what they *don't* want even if they may not be sure exactly what they *do* want. A short discussion of how the temp music is working can be revealing. It may also be the first step in negotiating a larger budget if necessary. For example, when asked what you think about the temp you might respond:

"I love it! Berlioz has always been a favorite of mine. Do we have that kind of budget? 'Cause I would love do that for you!"

Remember, the person who created the temp score may be in the room. Be gentle.

As for protocol, I like for the filmmakers to give me their ideas first. If I have a particular thought for a scene I'll say so, but I find the more I listen to the filmmakers the more I am able to ask questions and find a focus for their music.

Notice I said *their* music.

Some directors are really busy and have seen the picture so many times they prefer to jump from one scene to the next scene in which they know there will be a music cue. While you may have to honor this, I think the preferred method is to go straight through the movie, using a faster speed where there is no music immediately evident. You might find some source music, for example, that no one had thought about.

Each filmmaker will handle things a little differently so don't be shy. Ask how the filmmaker would like to proceed. You're attempting to appear experienced—not as if you're a mind reader. Experienced composers tend to ask more questions as they're aware of what things they're not expected to know.

SPEAK IN EMOTIONS

You'll hear this in every seminar and class you take on film scoring. That should tell you something. Encourage "drama speak" rather than musical references. You make the translation the same way the actor translates the writer's words and the director's instructions into a performance. The same way the director of photography translates the director's words into visuals.

Minor to you means lower the third a half step but to a non-musician it may merely mean "not sweet" or "not happy." These things can be accomplished in *major* as well. If you have to deal with a specific musical reference be very, very sure what is meant. Segovia, Eddie Van Halen, Ricky Skaggs and Keith Richards all play guitar. Twelve string or six? Gut, nylon or steel strings? Electric, acoustic, acoustic with a pickup or hollow body electric? With a pick? No pick? Fingerpicking? Bottleneck? Maybe dobro? Got a CD of what you've been listening to?

Oh! Hawaiian slack key guitar. Got it!

UNDERSTANDING THE NON-MUSICAL PEOPLE IN THE ROOM

It is common knowledge that everyone involved with a film sinks or swims with the finished product. We seldom if ever find a great score in a bad or mediocre film. No Academy nominations for costumes in a summer box-office flop. Therefore, there is an abundance of hopes and fears present in the spotting session. A lot of careers are looking to this production for a boost. In addition, while your music budget may seem small and insignificant, there have already been hundreds of thousands or maybe millions of dollars spent before you came on board.

Most filmmakers know something about almost all the elements involved in making a film. Without necessarily calling themselves experts, they have at least a familiarity with cinematography, writing, acting, directing, makeup, costuming, production financing, etc., but few know what a quarter note rest is.

If music (the mystery) was a part of early production, rather than postproduction, it would be far less intimidating. Early on there would still be time and money with which to fix or audition. But, with the film all but done and either working or not working and the delivery date lurking in the all too foreseeable future, it is not the best time to be adding an element which only one person in the room fully understands.

Or does he?

Everyone is hoping you will add a layer of brilliance to the film and at the same time they are terrified that you will absolutely destroy it.

SERVICING THE FILM

Many think that what we do is art. I disagree. Music is an art form. Film music is a craft with its roots in art. Art is a form of self-expression and the last thing a director wants is some composer coming in and expressing himself all over the director's film.

The tendency of film music students is to write their impression of the scene. When this happens, they are merely reiterating what the scene is already saying. We rather should be diagnosing what the scene needs to be saying and is not. If the scene is complete without music then there should be no music. This is what is meant by servicing the film. When you merely write your impression of the film, you are usurping the film for your own creative needs. Your inspiration.

HOW MUCH MUSIC?

The easiest mistake to make is to overwrite. The next easiest mistake is to underwrite. How do we know how much and where?

My personal method assumes that the perfect film is 100 percent complete. Not full—complete. There is a difference. A film is a collection of dramatic elements. Music and sound effects are added after many of those other elements are already in place. This allows us to assess how much of the job to be done actually has been done. Is this subjective? You betcha, but at least it represents a method of determining how much to write.

An example might be that the script, acting, lighting, direction, sets, cinematography, makeup and hair have all together created 80 percent of the desired effectiveness or completeness of the scene. It then falls to us (and sound effects) to add the final 20 percent. That might be a percussive rhythm, a wash or a high string note. More than 20 percent and the scene loses subtlety, robbing the audience of the fun of discovery. Less than 20 percent and we might leave the scene a little stark or raw or slow moving. Remember, it is certainly possible that all the other elements combined are doing 100 percent of the job required. When that's the case, as much as you would like to write some great music for that scene, it's time to stay away.

A GOOD QUESTION

The other side of that same coin is when the filmmaker suggests that "we should have music in here," and you not only disagree but have absolutely no clue as to what you would do.

Here are a couple of ideas. I find that if I first level with this person and say, "Gee, I'm not really hearing anything there," followed by, "What would the music be saying?" this does two things. The fact that I, the "expert," don't agree immediately softens the resolve, and the follow up asks him to explain what may have been just a guess or a whim. It is difficult enough to write a cue that does exactly what it's supposed to; writing music that has no purpose other than to placate the filmmaker is excruciatingly difficult. You will end up spending more time on that cue than on the ones that are really important.

If this tack doesn't work, then we have two other paths to try. We don't want to sit there and argue about it, so the next thing is to say, "Since I have no immediate feel for this cue, can I think about it and play with some things and we'll talk by phone later?"

This gives you a chance to do those very things. The filmmaker may be right and you may fully understand what's needed after spending a little time with the cue. On the other hand if you still can't see this as a necessary place for music, you can take the time to create your case and present it at a later time. Articulately.

Finally, realizing that it is not your film and that the possibility of working again with this person has indeed crossed your mind, you write something, making a mental note that when you go to the dub (final mix) you will suggest that they look at that scene without music and see if it needs the cue. This, by the way, will get you noticed and remembered by the dubbing mixers because no composer ever wants less music. Or so goes the myth.

Now let's reverse the situation. You think there should be music and the director disagrees. This is pretty easy, actually. You ask, "Do you mind if I write and record something for this scene and if it's not working for you at the dub, we'll just lose it?" Who is going to say no to someone offering them more than they've asked for—when they don't have to use it?

INS AND OUTS

"I'd like music here," my producer said with a significant degree of certainty. "I agree," I said, "but I don't think we want to hear it enter here."

Even the most serious student of film scoring can find it difficult to notice the beginning and end of every cue while watching a film. If the film is good, even we get caught up in the drama and forget to listen. If it's difficult for us, imagine how it is for someone whose first interest is not music. In the spotting session it may fall to you to prescribe a place to sneak in.

Cues that start and stop in the wide open spaces—between dialogue and with no sound effects to hide under—are risky at best and only work well in a stylized setting where the music is supposed to be noticed. Short cues in any other medium than sitcoms are generally to be avoided. I can best point out why by using massage as an example.

"Always keep at least one hand on the person once you start the massage."

This from a friend of mine who is a masseur. The reason is that the person relaxes and accepts the feel of your hands on their body. If you take both your hands away they will not only wonder why but anticipate when you are going to replace your hands. Will your hands be cold? Oily? Warm?

It's similar with music in film.

No matter how sneaky we are, the audience does, on some level, notice the music enter a scene. Because they've been to the movies before, their subconscious mind says, "It's okay, it's just dramatic underscore," and it is accepted as part of the audiovisual stimuli bombarding the brain. When the music stops it is also recognized by the brain. If this happens often it can constitute a distraction at least and an irritation at worst. If you have two scenes that require music separated by five or ten seconds, it might be wise to take the music where it can hang softly and out of the way between the two scenes (leaving one hand on the audience) rather than make two short cues with dead air in between.

THE OTHER SPOTTING SESSION

The second spotting takes place in our writing studio. It is the process of looking at each individual scene and diagnosing what is called for, where the sound effects or ADR might be and fine tuning entrances and exits. We'll cover this more in the next chapter.

CLOSING

The spotting session is over. This might be a good time for a bite to eat or a beer with the filmmaker. Sometimes the best insights come from more relaxed environments.

Tomorrow we set up and get ready to write!

Bellis and friend, director Charles Wilkinson. Mixing session at Bellis' studio in Santa Barbara, California.

CHAPTER FIVE

THE WRITING PROCESS

When it comes to composition I have always been fascinated by the concept of a muse. What is the muse and how does one "court the muse?"

A hint comes from the very definition of composition:

com·po·si·tion (käm´pe-zish´en) To put things in a particular arrangement; to organize elements in a particular way.

com·pos·ite (käm-poz´it) One thing made from assembling several individual elements.

The muse is the source of A.) things you know that you didn't know you knew, B.) the subconscious combining of seemingly unrelated ideas (as in a dream sequence) that then appear as an entirely new idea, and c.) the occasional tapping into a stream of consciousness by means not yet understood by physical science. Something one might describe as universal telepathy.

So, it would appear that the muse is a recycler.

Like any self-respecting mythological creature, the muse has an arch enemy. Or rather a group of conspirators who, when present, are able to successfully prevent her from putting in a appearance. These anti-muses are known as Anxiety, Insecurity and Panic—three states of mind to which all creative people are, at one time or another, subject. From what I know of film composers, they are often subject to all three on every project.

I have found over the years that courting the muse is actually a process of warding off the anti-muses. If one has a method of work that doesn't rely upon the muse, her ladyship is much more likely to show up.

CLEAR THE DECKS

Before you start working on a score, realize that it is a 24/7 job. Yes, I said 24. You will be dreaming the score. When you are eating, shopping, getting gas for the car, virtually every moment you will be thinking about the score. Some of this thought will be subconscious but it will be generating and formulating ideas as well as taking its toll on relationships.

"Sweetie, are you listening to me?"

So the first thing we want to do is anticipate anything that might interrupt the positive aspect of total immersion, and take care of it now.

That would include bills and any financial matters. Anticipate birthdays, anniversaries, graduations, soccer/T-ball games. Create a calendar specifically for this project period. Think about your daily work schedule.

> What is your most productive time of day?
> How many hours can you work continuously?
> When is the best time for "family time?"

Do you tend to work for long stretches at a time or take frequent breaks?

I am one of those frequent break takers and as such I find it helpful to refrain from A.) checking messages, B.) going into the family room, C.) turning on the TV, and D.) going near the refrigerator.

THE COMPOSER'S ASSISTANT

If you don't have a television series or aren't getting three major films a year, then your assistant is probably a part-timer. This position might be filled by a peer who isn't working at the moment, and you might want to reciprocate in kind when he has a project and you're available. This is especially true if it's a low-budget project.

This person could be an intern from one of the film and television music programs. It could even be your spouse, depending on your relationship. Talk it over first, this also has the potential to be significantly problematic. ("Honey, it's been three hours, do you mean to say you haven't written anything?")

Whatever you decide, an assistant is an important asset, probably even more important to the person with a family than it is for the single person. The assistant will actually increase the amount of time you have for your family.

Meet with Your Assistant

Set up your assistant's workstation away from your workstation. It's important to establish an "inner sanctum" into which few venture without good reason. If the assistant is too close it's too easy for you to ask, "Who was that on the phone?" or for the assistant to ask, "Do you want to speak to so-and-so?"

Show your assistant where everything is. Locate manuals, tech support phone numbers, instrument rental phone numbers, CDs and any research material he or you might need.

If purchases need to be made, will you reimburse him? Will he have access to a credit card or petty cash? How about IDs, passwords?

Will your assistant be doing any "music" work? Take downs, copying, orchestrating or ghosting cues? How will he be compensated for those tasks, as opposed to answering the phone and the other office tasks?

Figure out a work schedule for the assistant and suggest that he, too, "clear the decks" for the duration of the project plus 20 percent. You cannot be finding a sub or replacement and breaking in someone else during the project.

Bring your assistant up-to-date on names of the people with whom he might be dealing. Producers and directors deserve to be recognized when they call. Particularly if your assistant is going to say that you're "writing. Would you like me to interrupt him? He usually returns calls between 4 and 5 PM." Which brings us to the next bit of information your assistant will need.

Which calls get through at any time and which calls will you return when you take your "call back" break?

Have your assistant create a *contact list* with telephone numbers and email addresses.

Ask your assistant to program your speed dial phones, including the cell phones (his, too) with numbers you may need in the course of this project.

Let your assistant know how to back up important files and to what medium.

He should watch the film to become familiar with the character's names, major sequences, etc. This way if the director calls and leaves you a message about something that's being re-edited you can stop working on it and go on to something else.

He should be familiar with the deliverables including frame rate and sample rate.

Have your assistant create a work/flow chart with the name of each cue and at what stage of development it is. For example: *At* MIDI *translator. – At orchestrator. – At copyist.*

This chart can also include columns such as:
Preparing demo. – Signed off. – Requested changes. – Re-editing. – Waiting for visual effects.

Keep this current and you will always know exactly where everything is and how much is yet to be done.

Talk about the fact that the assistant's job is to take work away from the composer, giving you more time to write and think. As questions come up, suggest that he collect those questions and present them at a scheduled meeting with you.

If you're looking for work as an assistant, present some of these suggestions at your first meeting with a composer. That composer should be very impressed.

THE FORMATION OF THE WRITING METHOD

Step One - Getting in touch with reality

The film composer, writing against a deadline, needs to know that he will finish. On time. You cannot write brilliantly enough to offset showing up with an incomplete score.

The realization that we are not required to be totally original is the first step in being able to begin to write. I know, I know, every agent or studio exec you've heard speak at a seminar has talked about how "you have to find your own voice, blah, blah…" Well, why is it then that we keep hearing "Could you make it a little closer to the temp?" or "The temp is really original sounding, we want you to be original…just like the temp." Originality may be desirable to *get you noticed* but it's usually a different story once you're working on the project. "We really like that *Six Feet Under* theme." Don't look it up—it's Thomas Newman.

Film and television projects are made to be consumed by people. Folks. Plain ol' folks. Ordinary people. If originality is so important then why *King Kong, Mission Impossible, Father of the Bride*, etc., etc.? If originality is so important then why is so much importance given to test screenings? Are test audiences the arbiters of originality or are they actually more concerned that maybe there aren't enough explosions?

Film music serves most often to elicit a response from the audience member. An adrenaline rush, a moment of inner dread, a peaceful time, sadness. To *elicit* a response or *evoke* a feeling in someone, there must be at least a bit of recall involved. The music must be in some way reminiscent. It might be rhythmic or textural or melodic but something about it must "bring back" that original feeling or experience.

Yes, you will eventually put your "signature" on your music, but it is not imperative that the first note you write or enter into the sequence has never been thought of before.

I'm sure that in the so-called "Golden Era" of film score— the days of Korngold, Rózsa, Tiomkin and Herrmann— tongues were wagging at lunches and parties about how so-and-so stole that from Claude (Debussy) and "That's Tchaikovsky if I ever heard him."

Stanley Kubrick's *2001: A Space Odyssey* used "The Blue Danube," a waltz by Johann Strauss the Younger, composed in 1867. An original decision perhaps, but not an original sound.

Ladies and gentlemen: There are not only no pundits in our profession, there is no call for pundits. To profess "punditry" however, is rampant.

Step Two - Allocating your time

In my opinion, the biggest mistake you can make is to go home from the spotting session and start writing cues. Creating a score, on schedule and on budget, is like building a house; you must have a set of plans and a time line and abide by them. Yes, you can have changes, but the footprint of the house stays the same.

Here are the stages of writing to which I subscribe:

R & D: Research and development.

The Warm Up: Writing the cues for which you have an immediate idea.

The Meat: Writing the cues that are most important—to the filmmaker (first) and to the film (second).

The Follow Through: Writing the rest of the cues to finish the project.

Let's look at an example that involves six weeks.

R & D (*10 days to 2 weeks*)

This may seem like a long period of time which results in absolutely no cues written. The truth of the matter is that the more time you spend in this phase the faster and better the writing will be. Once you start thinking about a score you don't stop. You can be cooking, exercising, making love but you're still, somewhere in the back of your mind, thinking about that score.

I sit down and play the ideas, the fragments, every day—
two or three times a day. Inevitably, a tonality evolves and
after a few days, I've developed two or three (seemingly
unrelated) ideas. If I continue to play these ideas, they often
inform me how they might work together. Sometimes one
becomes an ostinato, working by itself and as an accom-
paniment for another idea. Often one evolves into a "B"
section of a theme.

The truth of the matter is that you will spend time in this
mode, whether it is now or later when you're trying to
compose a specific cue. The difference will be your frame
of mind. This is your creative time. Writing cues is your
crafting time. When you're writing cues you only want to
be opening your toolbox and selecting what you need, not
manufacturing new tools.

Because you are developing your musical ideas during this
period, it is also the time to create your sonic palette. If
you're working with melodies then you should be choosing the instrument or instruments that complement that
melody. If your thematic material is rhythmic then the
percussion family should be defined. This way, by the time
you start to write the cues you can set up a template in
the sequencing program or prepare your sketch pad for the
whole project.

It is important to make as many decisions as possible now,
before you start writing cues. The reason for this is economy. Time is the most precious thing you have. If absolutely
anything is possible then the choices become time con-

suming. Sooner or later you have to say "all right, it's going to be in the key of F, it's going to be in bass clef and it's going to be cello." You create parameters inside which your imagination can run free. A kind of musical corral if you will. Now you can go to work.

The Warm Up *(4 days)*
These are cues that I have an immediate idea or feel for. They are *not* the big cues of the project. These cues might be 40 seconds to two minutes but no more. This period of time is almost an extension of the developmental period because now that you are working to specific timings you might find the need to change a phrase or a time signature. This may further define and refine your thematic material.

The Meat *(2 – 3 weeks)*
Cues that have been designated by you and the filmmaker as important to the film are allocated a disproportionate amount of time. Sooner or later we must acknowledge a career mentality. You are servicing the filmmaker as well as the film. You cannot have a successful disagreement with the filmmaker. If you think, "I will do this my way and when the film airs or opens, people (including the director) will see that I was right," then you are delusional. Your score will never see the light of day. It will either be replaced or played so low and cut up into so many little pieces that you will not recognize it.

So, spend a great deal of time on this group of cues making them spectacular. This extra effort and extra time will yield so much material that...

The Follow Through (*balance of the time left*)

…will go very quickly indeed. This group of cues will be primarily derivative. Now, before you start thinking of derivative as a dirty word, let me remind you of continuity. A good word. This means that even if you have lots of different ideas, you might be better off using a select few, creating a palette, and achieving continuity.

In Chapter 2, I mentioned composing three minutes per day. This sometimes makes people crazy. They feel that if they only wrote 30 seconds the first day that they are already two and a half minutes behind going into day number two. Not true. What is really meant by this is an *average* of three minutes per day. By the time you get to The Follow Through period you will be writing seven, eight, nine minutes per day or more. That is how familiar you will have become with the material. You will be selecting from a toolbox full of quality tools and putting cues together in record time. All this speed, and continuity too. It's a beautiful thing.

THE SKETCH

John Williams is legendary within our community for his sketches. They are often 10 or 12 staves and totally complete. Probably a more accurate description of them would be a condensed score. The other end of the sketch spectrum might be what I call a layout sketch. One or two staves with descriptions of dramatic action and dialogue in their appropriate places. Additionally, it would contain time signatures, bar numbers and tempo markings—maybe no music at all. The John Williams sketch is going to be sent to the orchestrator and may very well end up on the podium where it will be used by John as he conducts (with fewer page turns than a full score). The layout sketch might be entered into a sequencing program.

People often don't consider the full purpose of the sketch and therefore don't feel they need one. Obviously, if you are working with an orchestrator you must give them something. A sketch with actual notes is, or should be, mandatory. The other reason for a sketch is that it provides you with an overview of the scene. By putting the dramatic elements on music paper you create an amalgamation of the drama and music.

A film unfolds one frame at a time. You can't see what has just passed or what's coming up. Your sequencer works in a similar fashion. While you are allowed to view more than one beat at a time, you are still limited as to how many bars you can watch scroll by in any given window. When you GO TO measure 56 you no longer can see measure 9. A sketch can let you see one or two minutes of drama at a time, in addition to all of your measures; all laid out on music paper *(see illustration on next page)*. You can decide what the time signature should be in order to make the music come out on a downbeat at the 146TH click. And you can start writing there if you so desire.

I find that being able to see the full length of the cue allows a much more linear style of scoring. The scene and the music seem cohesive because of dramatic leading. For example, after determining that the horse is going to break out of the starting gate at the 146TH beat, you start a small rhythmic fragment on beat 62 as the trainer and jockey exit the barn area. The fragment, in 12 beat increments, grows in complexity and presence, through the cellos and violas to the woodwinds and French horns, adding the percussion section until the tension of the horse being put in the starting gate (fidgeting, anticipating the gate opening) finally climaxes with the 146TH beat where the gates open, the bell rings and music hands off to live sound FX of the horses on the track. You're not scoring what's happening, but the *anticipation* of what's *going* to happen, and your sketch gives you a good long look at where you're going and where you've been.

Sketch from the television movie "One Special Night."

The practical use of even a minimal or layout sketch when sequencing becomes obvious to anyone who has tried to add beats or change time signatures once he has already put in a complete set of markers and some MIDI information. If, like me, you've been denied membership in the geek squad you can end up with an irreparable mess. This is a great time to be able to check against your layout sketch, which hasn't changed a bit.

PLAN "B"

There are times when we hear something in our head that we've never used or even heard anybody else use before.

"Is this too weird?"
"I wonder if the bass clarinet can play this."
"Should I go for it?"

Absolutely!

Just think about what you're going to do if:

The filmmaker hates it. "It's way weird."
The bass clarinet player can play it. Kinda. Sorta.

Don't count on being brilliant on the day of the session. Work out your Plan B now while there's no pressure.

FOR BETTER, FOR WORSE

When I was 15 years old I asked my dad, who was a music teacher, to give me some conducting lessons. He was always happy when I showed an interest in some new aspect of music, and so we started. After a couple of sessions in which I learned elementary beat patterns he said, "All right, now stand in front of this mirror and conduct in 4/4." I did.

"Bigger," he said. I did.

"Faster," he said. I did.

"Okay, stop. Did you hear that?"

"What?" I asked.

"Exactly. No matter how hard or fast you conduct, you can't make any music with your arms. Always respect the musicians."

This lesson applies not just to the musicians but everyone involved in turning your musical thoughts into audible music. The music editor, orchestrator, copyist, conductor, scoring mixer and the studio crew.

A lot can happen to your music on its way from your head to the ear of the audience. Changes from the original concept start when your finger hits a key or your pencil touches paper. A gossamer thought now has to be expressed using cumbersome tools and techniques. What was fluid is now divided into 8THS, 16THS and 32ND notes and what was unrestricted melody must now be confined to half steps, whole steps and multiple half-step intervals.

The more your musical thought is touched by others the more likely it is to change. Some for better, some for worse. Showing respect and concern for the next hands that touch your musical thought is the best way to ensure that the majority of those changes will be positive.

SHOW AND TELL

Sooner or later you will have to show the filmmaker what you've done. This is critically important if you are going to be scoring with live musicians. Getting cues approved or not is much more cost-effective at this mock-up stage than it would be with players sitting around waiting for you to work things out with the filmmaker.

No matter how many times you may have worked with this person or how much you believe she can envision what it's going to sound like when finished, do not skimp on quality for this demo session.

It is false economy to save time by throwing something together for the filmmakers to listen to. Even if they really are capable of imagining the finished cue (which no one except you can actually do), think how much more excited they will be if they don't have to imagine it.

I once played a few mock-ups for a couple of former students of mine. They had been working with me over the course of four or five years and both were thoroughly familiar with my music. This was a romantic comedy score that was going to be recorded with a modest-sized acoustic orchestra. Only after the recording session did they confess to me that when they heard the mock-ups, they were worried about the outcome.

If two fellow composers who are totally familiar with my work were worried, imagine how a (relatively) non-musical person, who might be working with me for the first time, would react. This was a real eye opener for me.

THE NEED TO CONTRIBUTE

For the last week, every time someone has called the film-maker's office asking about her availability on Thursday, the assistant has told them, "No, she's meeting with the composer on that day." She has set aside this time specifically for review of the proposed music for her film. It's likely that she will not come alone but maybe with one of the producers or the film editor.

It's show time. You have your assistant there to run the sequencer so that you can focus on comments. In addition, if there are any technical glitches, you can tap dance while your assistant works on the problem. You play the first cue and wow, you're a hero! "We sure got the right guy for this film," the director says and the producer readily agrees. Cue number two and, incredibly, the same slew of accolades.

Now, how long do you figure this can go on?

These people have put aside four hours or so to discuss the music. Will they just sit here and enjoy everything you've done for the next three and a half hours?

Not even if there was only one of them in the room, but certainly not if there are two or more. There exists in this room a need to contribute. Realize it, prepare for it and, most importantly, offer an opportunity for it.

> *"On this next cue, either the French horn, which would give us more warmth, or the English horn, which would give us a bit of despair, could be used for the melody. If it's okay with you, I'd like to play them both for you."*

Or, *"I think the high sparkle effect really works in this next cue but I'd be interested in your take on it."*

Otherwise, the comment will surely come during your absolute favorite cue and while it may be a good and relevant note, it might just as well be that it's merely time to make a contribution.

TIME FOR THE HAND OFF

On all but the lowest budget projects there comes a time when the composition leaves your hands and becomes the responsibility of someone else. This might be a MIDI translator, an orchestrator, a copyist, a synth person or a scoring mixer. Hopefully, you've given some thought to what that person will need to do his job and how you're going to deliver your music to him.

For example, if you're giving sequence files to a MIDI translator (someone who is going to turn your MIDI tracks into a sketch from which the orchestrator can work), try to have a consistent template so that in each file the instrument tracks or sounds are in the same location. If you're handing off to the orchestrator, give him the same package each time. That is, a sketch on the same paper, using the top line for certain instruments, the second line for other instruments, etc. Consistency allows people to establish a work routine of their own. The more time they spend figuring out what you did, the less time they have to do what they do.

Time, again.

I started arranging for bands when I was 13 years old. My first professional jobs were as an arranger and orchestrator. I love to orchestrate so when I started composing music for films I was not happy about the possibility that, due to shrinking deadlines, I might have to bring in someone to do orchestration. I thought I did it well and I enjoyed it, so how could I give it up? Then it finally hit me, if I had five weeks to compose and orchestrate a score I would have to divide my time into the two processes. I would compose for about three and a half weeks and orchestrate for the remaining 10 days. If I used an orchestrator, I could compose for five weeks and the orchestrator could orchestrate for five weeks. Which product would likely be better? This was a "no brainer."

When the instrumentation is small enough that I can adequately fit all the parts clearly onto sketch paper, I will, in effect, orchestrate as I compose and give the sketch to a trusted and experienced copyist.

The motto of a wise man I knew was "Take Partners." I am very grateful to Hank Mancini for sharing that wisdom.

CHAPTER SIX

RECORDING AND PODIUM PROCEDURE

"I don't want to make you nervous, but this session is costing a little over ten thousand dollars an hour."
—FROM A PRODUCER, FIVE MINUTES BEFORE MY DOWNBEAT

"We really need a recording order!"

This was voiced to me after the first three-hour session of my very first film. Oh, I had done plenty of recording before. All of it on tape either for records or television specials. This was my first film. Before that moment, no one had mentioned what havoc I was causing in the projection booth by not having a recording order. Projection booth? Yes, these were the days when the picture was projected on a big screen at the rear of the recording studio.

In those days, and thankfully this was about the end of those days, film music was recorded on 35 mm film stock that had been coated with magnetic stripes; just like magnetic tape but with sprocket holes. Using this format meant that all the sound elements—music, sound effects and dialogue—would run at exactly the same speed as the film; 24 frames a second. At the dub, or final mix, the elements were put on "dummy" machines (35 mm projectors without the light or lens; just a sound head) and if one element was out of synch, that machine would be taken "off line," the film stock advanced or retarded, put back on line and—taa daa!—you had perfect synch again.

I had a lot to learn back then. For example, the picture was divided into 10-minute reels. The term "a ten reeler" referred to this system of ten, 10-minute reels of film. Who knew? Since we were recording to picture, these ten reels were sitting on a rack in the projection booth. Had I given everyone a recording order, the projectionists, while running the scene for the current cue, would have been able to prepare for the next cue to be recorded. Instead, they were waiting for me to call the next cue number from the podium. If that cue wasn't on the current reel, they would take that reel off the projector, put the next reel on the "bench" and roll down to the start mark, put it on the projector and fire it up. All the time they're thinking "!@#*^!?@%^*!!" and all the time I'm thinking, "What could be taking so long?"

I'm not sure if we went into overtime that day but I'd be surprised if we didn't. It was, however, in the days when the composer was given a fee for the composition, and all production expenses (including recording studio, musicians, orchestration and copying) were paid by the production company or studio. It is even more important to be efficient today, when the vast majority of the work is "package" work.

To a large extent, efficiency is knowing what to expect and planning for it. The whole point of reading and studying to be a film composer is to gain experience vicariously, making you appear to filmmakers more experienced than you actually are.

PODIUM VS. BOOTH

You can't be in two places at once. Since you have to pick either the podium or the booth, the easy decision would be to choose the one for which you are most qualified, and for most emerging composers that would unquestionably be the booth. All the composers I know agree that there are advantages to both.

Political Advantages
The booth has the advantage from a "putting out fires" point of view. You can explain concepts and defuse worries at the speed of speech.

The political benefit to being on the podium is one of perception. You are leading a large and talented group—similar to the way the director leads while on the set. This gives you something in common. Something impressive.

In addition, these world-class musicians are looking to you and asking questions of you. This represents a position of respect and power. It is also the very thing that scares the s_ _ _ out of many emerging composers.

Musical Advantages

The composer/conductor on the podium is immediately available to the musicians for questions. They will ask much more freely than if their question must go through a surrogate and be relayed into the booth for an answer. In addition, the composer can ask discreet questions of the musicians: "Is the trill awkward in that register?"

Not that any of us make silly mistakes, but if one ever did, it would be much easier to quietly fix it from the podium rather than trying to create a "talkback code" that camouflages any admission of error on our part.

The composer in the booth hears the music in a sonically superior environment and has the flexibility to immediately change the balance if something is offensive to the filmmaker.

My feeling is that: A.) If you can do it, then you can farm it out. Be able to conduct and then *decide* to give it away and B.) If the circumstances dictate, you should be able to do either. That is to say, if you are having a difficult relationship with the filmmaker, be in the booth; if the filmmaker doesn't come to the session, be in the live room with the musicians.

Some combinations can work as well. If you choose to stay in the booth, have a conductor but go into the live room yourself for rehearsals. If you are on the podium, take as many opportunities as time permits to go into the booth and confer. Finally, a third possibility that some filmmakers actually enjoy: Bring them into the live room with you for the rehearsal.

Why Hone Podium Procedure?

First of all, *podium procedure* is not just conducting. Conducting is a component of podium procedure, but I consider podium procedure to be everything you do while in charge of the recording session.

The primary reason to hone these skills is to create an efficient, smooth-running and pleasant session. Here are a few other reasons, in no particular order.

Gain the respect of the orchestra

The musicians are not looking at the score. Nor have they seen the film or heard your demos. They are looking at one cue at a time and one part of that cue—their part. The way you handle yourself and the session affects what the musicians think of your music. If you are hard to hear, hard to understand and difficult to follow, attitudes will deteriorate over the course of the day. It might very well be that the last 20 minutes of the session is when you most need their help and cooperation.

Be able to vary the performance

Both for stylistic and pragmatic reasons, the ability to conduct and have the players follow you is a definite advantage. Let's say there has been a change in the picture since you spotted it or the variable click that you created was accidentally deleted. You know the music for this scene better than anyone else. Rather than waiting for a technical fix or trying to explain it to your conductor, you might be able to conduct that cue free time and move on with your session. (And there is always the possibility that your conductor might get stuck in traffic or have to attend to an emergency.)

Be able to write free time

Conducting is one of the secrets to writing well in free time. The ability to conduct the music at your writing table or workstation while you sing it, makes for the most graceful and musical cues. After listening over and over to your own variable click, you can become so accustomed to it that it doesn't seem jarring anymore—to you! But how will 10, 20, 30 or more players react?

As opposed to creating a variable click or playing along with picture and *making* it work, when you conduct as you write, you are assured that the entire orchestra will be able to follow the changes in tempi.

Be able to concentrate

Except for the most seasoned conductors, when one steps up on the podium, there is a rush of adrenaline. Unfortunately, the abiliy to concentrate is negatively impacted by this rush. This is why we discover those wrong notes in the woodwind section when we're listening to the mix four days after the session.

Part of the reason for this lack, or rather loss, of concentration is insecurity. We are thinking about our performance. After all, we're standing in front of people who have been playing their instruments since they were in elementary school and we've been conducting for how many hours now? Okay, that may be an exaggeration, but however long we've been conducting, it is likely not nearly as long as they have been playing. We, the least experienced, are being called upon to lead. And not only to lead but to answer questions; questions about the musicians' parts, complete with transpositions.

A number of things at the session demand our attention concurrently:

> *Is the music lining up correctly with the picture?*
> *Is it working dramatically with the picture?*
> *Was that a mistake I just heard in the harp part?*
> *Five four bar coming up!*
> *Lunch, coming up!*
> *I must remember to tell the booth about the percussion switch from vibes to cymbals in bar...ouch! I guess they know now.*

The secret of success here is making some of the tasks, the ones that are common to every session, automatic. Having several *mini routines* is a good way to start. Here's an example of one of mine:

Whether getting ready to make a *take* or a rehearsal, I use the same routine to count off each cue. Having played in bands and orchestras while growing up, I know that every young musician is taught that when the conductor's arms go up it means "instruments up!" If I had the undivided attention of everyone in the orchestra, all I would have to do is raise my arms, but in a television or film session people are making notations on their parts, fixing accidentals, working out bowings and deciding how they're going to change doubles, so I add a simple voice command as I raise my arms: "Here we go."

As you know, there is a warning streamer that takes two seconds to cross the screen from left to right. When this streamer hits the right edge of the screen the countoff or warning clicks start.

I look for a SMPTE number or a place in the scene about five seconds before the yellow warning streamer appears. I raise my arms and say, in my best public speaking voice, "Here we go! Eight for free!" The musicians can't see the yellow streamer and consequently have no idea when the first of the warning clicks will sound so, when the yellow streamer is about halfway across my monitor screen I say, "Annnnnnd," and as the streamer hits the right edge of the screen, I start my count off of the warning clicks, "One, two, three…" I will do this exactly the same way for all 30 or 40 cues. The players become accustomed to it and that makes it easy for them to know when they have to bring the instruments up and prepare to play. I can concentrate on other things because this part of my job has become automatic.

You can also automate your basic conducting patterns so that they don't require any conscious thought. Golfers, basketball players and many other athletes count on muscle memory for consistency in their game. We can do the same with conducting. More on this later.

Before the Recording Date
There are so many things that we must keep track of at the session that any potential distractions should be dealt with beforehand.

The deadline
You should consider two days before the session day as your writing deadline. This should give you much of the day before the date to do whatever work has spilled over, prepare your materials and yourself for the scoring session and most importantly, get a full night's rest. I try to schedule my sessions for the latter part of the work week; Wednesday, Thursday or Friday. This way I can work like crazy over the previous weekend and the copyists have at least two, full, non-overtime days to finish up before the session.

Preparation: musical and otherwise
Go over each score and mark those places for which you might need a visual aid: time signatures, Plan B, free time, warning clicks, anything. This also gives you a look at some of the cues you last saw about three weeks ago.

Pack up your tools: stopwatch, pocket metronome, highlighter, pencils, eraser, blank manuscript paper, etc. Be sure to have telephone numbers of your contractor, copyists, mixer, producer and director.

Don't forget personal items: deodorant; toothpaste, breath mints, medications. Those things that will help keep you from feeling uncomfortable or self-conscious.

Pick out what you're going to wear. If you are going to conduct, remember that you will be physically active *and* nervous. Pick something comfortable, cool, stylish and functional.

Prepare for the stress and pressure. How will you handle the chronic negativity of a certain someone?

Who might be there? Be sure you know the names. Also any pertinent events like the recent death of a parent or the graduation of a daughter or son. Remember, no one except you is totally consumed with what is going to be happening today. Life is going on all around you.

Feign normalcy.

Finally, just give some thought to anything that might shake your concentration. Try and deal with it now or prepare for it happening at the session.

Starting the Session
Here's that four-letter word again: Time.

Be on time. For the composer that should be *no less than* 30 minutes before the downbeat. There will be questions and there may be problems that require you to shift gears. The copyist may have made some red question marks on the score you handed in yesterday; you should take a look. If, miracle of miracles, there isn't anything that needs your attention, review your scores or go schmooze somebody.

At two minutes to the downbeat the contractor will take the podium and announce, "Ladies and Gentlemen, good morning. This is a film session for XYZ Productions and our composer this morning is…" The orchestra will start to tune and…

You take the podium.

First things first. Calm yourself! Keep that adrenaline rush at bay.

You say, "Good morning. First of all, I want to let you know who is lurking in the booth. Our mixer this morning is…" and you start your introductions. The scoring mixer, score reader, orchestrator, soloists (if any) and the music editor. Even if the players are unfamiliar with your work, the company you keep should help signify that this is going to be a professional session. Additionally, the musicians may be dealing with these people directly while you're busy doing something else.

PHOTO BY LESTER COHEN/WIRE IMAGE

Bellis on the podium of the Newman Stage on the Fox lot.

Ready for Rehearsal

Give the name of the cue and any general information (they don't need to know the backstory of how the woman and her daughter got to Pennsylvania after her husband died in ww2).

I like to be giving an approximate tempo with small beats of my baton while I'm waiting for picture or giving last-minute instructions. This lets the musicians have a realistic look at their parts knowing what the approximate tempo will be. The final bit of information you'll give the musicians will be how many clicks "for free" (warning clicks) there will be.

Ask your music editor for the picture; five seconds before the yellow streamer, "Here we go…Eight free.…Annnnd one, two, three, four, five…."

While the musicians are perfectly capable of counting to eight by themselves, the idea behind your count is that all clicks sound alike; counting the first few clicks will ensure that everyone started counting on the same click.

Generally, we allow two measures of warning clicks unless the tempo is slow, in which case one measure should be fine. Never finish the count. Always leave at least the last two counts silent.

TIP: The podium is really a big hollow box, usually covered with carpet. If you tap your foot or are just a mover and shaker on the podium, you could be adding something that will sound like mezzo-piano bass drum throughout every cue. At least take your shoes off (add clean socks to your preparation list).

REHEARSAL

Experience will give you a pretty good idea of which mistakes will be corrected on the second play-through and which should be mentioned now. If unsure, give the players the benefit of the doubt. Don't hesitate to take credit for your own "clams." Nobody's perfect—especially composer/conductors.

Questions, Questions

Ask the musicians if they have questions.
Ask them how the click level was.
Anyone need more or less volume?
Ask the mixer if there is anything—a section, a certain instrument—that he would like to hear.
"Are we ready to rehearse again?" directed at the booth.
Another rehearsal and you're ready for a *take.*

Addressing the Musicians

The contractor will usually be happy to supply a list of all the musicians' names and instruments. If you want to address individuals, a name is the best way to go. Everyone likes to be recognized.

When speaking to sections, you pretty much have to use the name of the instrument, however, it's a good idea to focus on the principal player. In most sections this is a courtesy but with the violins, it's downright mandatory. You address the concertmaster and she will either relate or translate to the section.

When speaking to the entire orchestra, I prefer "Ladies and Gentlemen."

No matter who you are addressing, the most important thing is to speak up! It's fatiguing when one has to strain to hear the conductor. And the larger the orchestra the more the musicians will have to strain. After a few hours this will take a toll on attitudes, or worse, they will merely stop straining.

The orchestra setup for recording spreads out the players much more than they would be for a concert. In addition, there will be gobos, moveable walls of glass and/or sound insulation, placed between you and some of the sections. Yes, they can hear you in their headsets *if* they are wearing them and *if* your mic is turned on. Don't chance it. Speak up.

Making Changes/Fixes

If you say "bar 56" everyone in the orchestra looks at bar 56.

Then you say "the F#" and everyone scans their notes in bar 56 for an F#.

Finally you say "for piano" and everyone except the piano player goes back to what they were doing. The acceptable "address" for a change or fix is WHO, WHERE and WHAT.

"Piano…bar 56, beat 4…F *natural*"

Take your time and get it right before giving a change to the musicians. They're not fond of erasing and moving changes once you've given them out.

Should you have to dictate a rhythmic figure, you might want to check your dictation by singing it to the appropriate player or section. This can be one of the few "right" times to sing a figure. Don't forget to count it off so that everyone knows where the downbeat is.

Ask, "Can we have an 'A' please?"

Now, they took an "A" before the session started but another one will be needed before the take. You may not require another for the rest of the hour. When needed, I usually ask for an "A" after the rehearsal(s) but before the first take of each hour. This has nothing to do with playing out of tune. Air conditioning and humidity do their thing at every session.

CONDUCTING—THE MOVES

If you have taken courses in conducting or have conducting experience you still may want to rethink some of your moves for the recording studio. If you have never conducted or were perhaps an assistant conductor in high school, you will find that with just a little practice you can do just fine at the session. Don't feel apologetic about your conducting. You have written all the music and have landed a job that results in all these people having work. That's already enough to earn you the respect and gratitude of the players and technicians gathered to produce this music.

Realize that your input can be verbal as well as visual. The directions you give during rehearsal more than justify your presence on the podium. You can probably get away with a good countoff and an even better cutoff.

At a recording session the conductor is conducting sight reading. This is different than conducting a concert piece in which the orchestra has become accustomed to your conducting style during multiple rehearsals. It is more akin to what a concert conductor will do while rehearsing a particular section of a piece. For a concert conductor this might be considered "marking" (from marking time). It's conducting without the tuxedo.

Plenty of books and internet sites show diagrams of the basic moves. If you learn the moves for 2/4, 4/4, 3/4 and 5/4 you'll have almost everything you'll need. 6/4 can be a 4/4 pattern and a 2/4 pattern or a 2/4 pattern and then a 4/4 pattern depending on how the music is phrased. 7/4 is a 3/4 pattern followed by a 4/4 pattern or a 5/4 pattern and a 2/4 pattern and so on.

Here are some of the most important points:
The downbeat goes *downward.* In the middle of the body (to about the diaphragm). Don't make it so low that the players can't see the bottom of your beat behind the podium desk.

The last beat of each bar goes up from the right side (approximately four o'clock) to the starting point for the next downbeat (12 o'clock). The next to last beat is always out to the right. These remain the same regardless of the time signature.

Have a distinct snap or bounce at the bottom of each beat (even in free time).

While it may be counterintuitive, if you want the orchestra to go faster make your beat smaller and closer to your face; if you want them to slow down make your beat bigger and broader.

While recording to click, if *you* screw up, don't stop. You'll never hear it.

Conduct primarily with your right hand (even if you're left-handed).

Mirror with the left hand only for changes in time signatures and other similar areas of importance.

Left hand can be used for dynamics, clarity of downbeats in multiple time signatures, ritardandos and accelerandos, cutoffs and cues.

Cue an entrance only if you plan on doing so each time. The player may come to rely upon your cue.

"On the stick" refers to notes played one at a time as the conductor gives a downbeat for each. This is done primarily to check for wrong notes.

No foot tapping—no humming.

In free time the upbeat or preparatory is the only indication of tempo the orchestra will get. Make sure you know the tempo before you start.

Make sure that the individual beats are in very distinct positions so that a player who looks up in the middle of the bar will know exactly what beat you're on.

After the cutoff, keep your arms raised and turn your palms toward the orchestra. This will help keep it quiet for those few important seconds of ring off.

Speaking of cutoffs, people who are learning to drive need to know how to stop before they put the car in motion. This is a good idea for conductors as well. The cutoff should have a definite abrupt end that indicates to the players a moment when all sound must cease. An easy cutoff is simply a counterclockwise circle with the right hand that takes one beat to execute and starts and finishes at the same point of the circle (approximately five o'clock). Mirror this action with your left hand.

A BIT OF ADVICE

A trumpet player may be able to hit a "G" above high "C" but his actual, usable range might be a third below that. It is the same with conductors. If you expect to be able to conduct, run the session, make changes and hear mistakes, pitch problems, etc., you must be overqualified for the conducting job at hand.

This applies to all aspects of our work. If you want to move up in this business, you must appear to be doing work that stands above the present assignment. Work at being overqualified. Learn and practice more than you need to know. Overqualified means that you'll have to concentrate a little more to avoid careless errors. Barely or under-qualified means you will be in a perpetual state of panic. Maybe *almost* overqualified is the optimum target.

Finally, there is this consideration for the filmmaker at the session:

BIG MUSIC, LITTLE PICTURE

This is the atmosphere in the recording studio. It is 180 degrees away from what the filmmaker is envisioning as the final result.

In those days, to which I referred earlier, when the picture was projected on a big screen (albeit a B&W work print), it was a little easier to see and hear things in perspective. Now that we are viewing on a television monitor and listening on big studio monitors, the composer would be wise to give the filmmaker a chance to hear a playback with dialogue up and music mixed low enough to resemble the final mix. Do this early in the session to help the filmmaker get through the rest of the day without feeling that she has to keep asking for things to be taken out and parts to be played softer.

PHOTO BY LESTER COHEN/WIRE IMAGE

Richard Bellis with Sean Paxton—ASCAP Television & Film Scoring Workshop.

CHAPTER SEVEN

DELIVERY AND THE DUB

"You never actually finish mixing, you just stop."
RAY COLCORD, COMPOSER

If there were a Love Index Meter with which to rate each of the tasks a composer must perform, I think it would be safe to assume that the high scorer would be creating the music. On the other hand, preparing the music elements (deliverables) for the dub or final mix would probably not register very high at all. We seldom finish writing early just so we'll have plenty of time to prepare elements.

I like the word *pristine* when it comes to describing deliverables. Let me put it another way. Let's say that you're in a serious automobile accident on your way to the dub. While you're en route to the hospital, unconscious, someone finds your mangled car, digs out the DVD on which the final Pro Tools session lives, takes it to the dubbing stage where they load it in the computer and voila!—everything is clear and understandable. Absolutely pristine! It won't be necessary to call your assistant for the backup copy you left with her or download anything from the ftp site where it also exists—just in case.

Obsessive/compulsive? Anal retentive?

You bet! And with good reason.

THE DUB OR FINAL MIX

This is the most important place your music will ever be heard. Bar none. Not just because the director and producers will be there or because the music may, from time to time, be played without any sound effects. To fully understand, we have to review what actually happens in the final mix. The goal of the final mix is to assemble all the audio elements of the film, balance, mix and marry them to the picture. The audio elements involved are divided into three general categories. Dialogue, effects and music. The elements consist of:

Production Dialogue
Dialogue that was recorded during principal photography.

ADR *(Automated Dialogue Replacement a.k.a. Additional Dialogue Replacement or Alternate Dialogue Replacement)*
Dialogue recorded in a studio during postproduction. The actors perform their replacement dialogue while watching their original performance. Production sound might be

unusable due to the location noise or conditions. ADR is also used to describe new dialogue which might be added to enhance the story. In this instance the dialogue comes from an unseen source or an actor who has his back to the camera.

Walla
Background conversations recorded in postproduction and specifically tailored to each scene. Recorded by a voice-over group.

Voice-Over
Narration that was not a part of the production sound.

Sound Effects
Sounds selected from a library of sound effects and assembled for each scene.

Custom Effects
Sometimes called designer effects. These are sounds created for a specific element of the story. For example, an inanimate object such as an "angry room."

Foley Effects
Effects recorded by sound effect "actors" to replace or enhance the actions in the scene. The footsteps of an actor walking on carpet may not be audible enough on the production track, for example.

Music Score
You should probably be familiar with what this is.

Source Music
This is music that is coming from a source, either seen by the camera or imagined to be in the vicinity.

The dubbing stage is like a full-service hospital for audio. There are births (creative ideas), deaths (of ADR, foley and music cues), emergencies (equipment failures, missing sound elements), treatments (laborious sound processing) and politics ("There's nothing I can do, the music is fighting the dialogue."). There are doctors (the mixers, music editor and FX editor), patients (mostly production sound), loved ones (the composer and the director who occasionally shed a tear over the dearly departed) and nervous parents (the producers).

The main difference between a hospital and a dubbing stage is that there is no insurance to help cover the cost of the dubbing stage. These rooms, fully staffed, will run from a low of $500 per hour to over $1,500 per hour and, believe me, there are no speed records broken in dubbing.

Can you feel the tension starting to build?

The dubbing stage is a dark place. Some days darker than others. It is quiet, as people are carefully listening. And the entire environment is sonically treated, so it feels even quieter.

Dubbing Stage. Euphonix console on Stage 7 at Todd-AO West.

Quiet, dark, slow-moving and expensive. So, why would a composer want to be there? A large percentage of what is accomplished in the dub can only be referred to as problem solving: processing problematic production sound, moving or replacing sound FX, remixing the music stems because one instrument is objectionable for some reason, finding the "looped" line that the line producer swears he recorded but now seems to have vanished.

Most problems are solved satisfactorily, but once in a while, either when there is no acceptable solution or the clock has already been running a little too long, the team is forced to infer blame. Blame, when not obvious, most often follows the path of least resistance. The mere presence of the composer increases the resistance level of the path known as the "music department." The music editor will fight for you, but she didn't write the music so the language used to describe the perceived musical problem will be much different if you are in the room. For example:

Situation 1: No composer present.
In a loud voice, "Jeez, what is that music doing?"

Situation 2: Composer in the room.
In a much softer voice, "Richard, when we roll back can we talk about that cue?"

The first situation will increase everybody's awareness *and suspicion* of the music in the *rest of the movie.* The second situation makes the composer part of the solution team. One negative, the other positive.

In Chapter 4, I mentioned that the spotting session was one of a couple of times that you would be spending a considerable amount of time sitting next to the filmmaker. This is the other. The dub might be three days or three weeks long. If it's the former, you may want to be there all day, every day. A lot of music will go by each day and you'll get a chance to have at least one meal with the filmmaker. On a three-week or longer dub, some of the days won't involve music at all, while others may be just music. The crew may decide to pre-dub the dialogue or spend a day or two just doing the FX. Check in by phone in the morning or stop by about a half hour before lunch to see if you can join the lunch crowd.

Another, important reason for being at the dub is quality control. Here again, the music editor will stick up for you but you may be the only one who really knows what that particular sample should sound like, or if the stereo reverbs are reversed.

I would say, conservatively, that on 70 percent of the dubs I've attended, some technical happening affected the music and had to be corrected. These problems included: only the electronic elements playing, with the orchestral tracks nowhere in sight; only one side of the stereo image being heard; the stereo reverbs being reversed. Cues could be in the wrong location. They might be in the right location but after seeing and hearing everything together you might decide that the cue should start 10 frames later so as to clear a particular sound effect or ADR.

THE "THROW AWAY" CUE

The first 30 to 40 minutes of any score are usually easy and fun to write. It's the last 20 minutes that get challenging. Of course, once you've written the wonderful, important cues, it's tempting to take some pressure off yourself by diminishing the importance of the last few cues.

One such writing moment ended up teaching me a painful lesson. The cue was only 37 seconds in length. I was very happy with the cues I had completed for the film so far and this little, seemingly unimportant cue was in the last 10 minutes of the picture. I was sure that no one would be paying any attention to it, so I gave it far less time than it deserved.

While I was probably correct about its importance to the film, I did not anticipate what would happen in the dub.

When there is a problem with production dialogue and an ADR line has been recorded to replace it, the dialogue mixer must spend a significant amount of time matching the ADR line to the line recorded in production. The new line was recorded in a recording studio, sometimes in the location where the actor is working on his or her next film. The ambient sound of the new line has to match the ambient sound of the location where the original production line was recorded. This can be a long process and often, after 15 or 20 minutes, the filmmaker will say, "You know what? Let's listen to the original line again. This ADR line just doesn't have the same energy." With that, the dialogue mixer will try to "dig out" the original line using filters and other voice processing equipment. This takes another 15, 20, 30 minutes or more.

The process involves making a loop of the troubled dialogue. Normally, this is just a dialogue loop but in some cases, the mixer might decide to "drag along" the music and effects in order to hear the environment in which the dialogue will have to be heard. Guess which cue of mine accompanied just such a scene. The one that I "threw away" of course. I had to sit through an interminable amount of time hearing it repeated, and I couldn't distract attention using witty conversation because the mixer had to listen closely to the dialogue. Over and over and over again. Stupid, stupid, stupid cue. Lesson learned and now passed along.

Which brings up a related subject.

THE LESS-THAN-WONDERFUL CUE

"I'm not sure that you need music here at all. Why don't we just see it once without the cue?"

These words, uttered by a composer on the dubbing stage, are guaranteed to create A.) at least 10 seconds of silence in the room while people decide how to respond, and B.) a legend that will be passed from dubbing mixer to dubbing mixer for years to come.

After all, it is well-known that if you have a composer in the dub, all that composer wants is for the music to be louder. This is, or should be, myth. The truth of the matter is that the composer, along with everyone else whose work is represented in the film, succeeds or fails based on the success or failure of the film in its entirety. Therefore, it is in our best interest to advocate whatever is best for the film.

Now, I'm sure you've never written a "less-than-wonderful" cue, but I have. So, just in case you ever do, this method can be the way to not only lose that cue but establish yourself as a (seemingly) selfless, team player. Then, in reel 7 when you want to hear the music louder, people will be much more likely to oblige—assuming it's appropriate of course.

Often, in an effort to keep from offending the composer, someone who thinks the cue is not working will ask for the cue to be lowered in volume rather than suggesting that it be taken out completely. Though the person may have good intentions, this suggestion won't make a poorly written cue sound better, and in fact a well-written cue played too softly will sound bad. So compromise isn't always the best answer in filmmaking. For the good of the film, it's either this or that, in or out, right or wrong.

While your music sounded great and worked perfectly in your office, the dub can change all that. It will now be competing for sonic space with elements that you had not heard before. And, the cues themselves may need to be moved by a few frames or to an entirely new location in the film.

Be there!

PHOTO: ED KALNINS

Todd-AO West dubbing stage.

CHAPTER EIGHT

RANDOM THOUGHTS

ON NEGOTIATION

Many people love their work. Some are even as passionate about their work as composers are. Every occupation encompasses multiple and varied tasks, some which are pleasing and others which are merely a necessary price for enjoying the pleasant ones. We often are much more proficient at those tasks we enjoy and do a significantly poorer job on the more unpleasant ones.

Some of the tasks and roles attached to the occupation of film composer might be: *composer, orchestrator, mixer, copyist, music editor, conductor, producer, negotiator, agent, public relations, and bill collector.*

Several things on this list would qualify as our least favorite things to do. Negotiation is often one of them. We intuitively try to give this job away, realizing that in order to be a strong negotiator we have to be willing to let the *deal* fall through. This makes us extremely uncomfortable because it could keep us from doing the task we love: composing the music.

For the emerging composer, getting an agent to do the negotiations for you might not be an option. You may find yourself negotiating with an attorney or worse, a legal department.

Attorneys, too, have tasks that they like and dislike. Unfortunately, they like—maybe even love—negotiation. We are doing a task we don't do well while they are doing a part of their job that they love to do. To add to our discomfort, if we let this offer go, a dozen or more people are out there waiting to take whatever was offered. This is a negotiation disaster waiting to happen. What can we do? Several things.

First, look into composer contracts. All of them may appear to be different, but actually they are very similar. They all contain categories such as:

Services: What you are expected to do.
Compensation: What you will receive in exchange for what you are expected to do.
Credit: How and where your name will be presented.

These and several other categories comprise all composer contracts. There will be language on ownership and royalties, publishing and soundtracks, and in the United States, a Certificate of Authorship assigning the copyright to the production company. The main difference will be in the number of words and pages. Generally, the larger the legal department, the more words. The need to contribute reaches all professions.

A lawyer (not my current lawyer) once said to me after I questioned some aspect of a contract, "You don't want to learn legalese." I laughed it off and went home without my answer. On the way home it occurred to me that if I could learn how to read and write music, I should not have too much difficulty learning at least enough legalese to understand a contract. That goes for all of us. You don't have to want to be a lawyer to learn what your contract says.

Speaking of attorneys, get one. A "music" attorney.

"But they're soooo expensive," we whine. No they're not. Sample libraries are expensive. Computers are expensive. These things will be outdated in 18 months. If you treat an attorney as a teacher and not just a service provider, you can get an education in composer/music law for a lot less than they had to pay for it. And, it will stay valid for years if not decades.

Yes, attorneys have a pretty healthy hourly fee, but they often charge in 10-minute increments. In today's marketplace, an attorney is as valuable as any piece of studio equipment you may have.

Talk over hypothetical negotiations with your attorney so that when an opportunity for work presents itself, you won't have to worry and struggle with what things you might offer or negotiate for, you'll already have a plan for that scenario that merely requires a little tweaking to fit the current situation.

Create your own contract, complete with everything the production company requires. The production company might insist on using its composer agreement, but it normally takes the company a very long time to generate that agreement. Sometimes you won't see the agreement until after the work is done.

As soon as you are told you have the job, send off your contract. Now they have it in hand. You or your attorney can almost *red line* their agreement over the phone by comparing sections of the two agreements. Put in some items you would be willing to negotiate away.

The party who makes the initial offer always has the edge. In tic-tac-toe who has the advantage? When a baseball bat is thrown up and caught by the handle, the last one to "cap" it is the winner. The person who grabs first can estimate the distance but each subsequent hand that grabs is at the mercy of the first hand. When you bargain for something at a yard sale, you use the price marked on the item as a starting point. That initial price may be inappropriately inflated but that is where the bargaining starts. Sending off your own contract gives you an edge. Slight or significant. Small production companies might not even have a composer agreement and would need to hire an attorney to draft one. They would probably much prefer to have counsel read and red line an agreement rather than draft one.

We are small businesses. We should expect and accept expenses such as promotion, communication, transportation, shipping and legal. We often think of ourselves as artists. That's fine at the appropriate time (at our writing stations), but will not serve us well while doing the craft or business aspects of our profession.

Finally, there are a couple of crucial points that are not necessarily in the so-called "standard" composer agreement. The first is that you must receive a copy of the cue sheet. This is the only way you have of knowing if the information upon which your royalties will be based is correct. It also lets you know that a cue sheet *has* been created. In the event that you don't see the title of this film showing up on your statements a year after the movie aired on television or opened overseas, you can inquire with your PRO (Performing Rights Organization) and, if necessary, submit a copy of the cue sheet yourself.

The second point is that the music you write for this film must not be used in any other film without negotiation in good faith. Because the production company will likely own this music, you don't want it creating a music library and essentially putting you out of business with your own music.

ON THE CRAFTSMAN'S ATTITUDE

Composing music is a form of expressing oneself. Art. Composing media music is a collaborative craft. You are at best an artisan and quite often a craftsperson. You are creating a mere aspect of the whole production the same way lighting, costuming and cinematography function in concert to create the final, single entity. When you compose for the concert stage, it is permissible to be satisfied with what you've written even if it gets bad reviews and proves to be non-revenue-producing. A film composer who writes wonderful music that fails to service the picture, however, relinquishes the right to self-satisfaction. That composer has endangered the professional reputations of all those connected with that production, not to mention perhaps millions of company dollars. Your obligation is to do what's right for the project, whether or not you find it to your personal liking.

ON DESPERATION

If you are not independently wealthy, do not have a rich uncle, have not saved enough to support yourself for two or three years…then get a job. Emerging composers who are getting financially desperate are a threat not only to themselves but to the community. They will negotiate bad deals that will result in poor performances and set precedents with filmmakers.

The best job to find is as an assistant to a working composer. The next might be as an orchestrator, copyist or MIDI translator. After that, working in an associated field: for a music publisher, a composer's agent or a PRO.

If none of the above are available to you, then you might want to find a job that gives you at least some of your daytime hours free for phone calls, meetings and lunches.

Having a source of revenue with which to meet your financial responsibilities will keep desperation from becoming part of your everyday persona.

IS THERE TOO MUCH "U" IN YOUR MUSIC?

Whenever you write something of which you are particularly proud, or something you feel is absolutely perfect for a scene, you are creating a potential liability. As soon as that cue is questioned, not accepted, not appreciated, or changed, your attitude changes. Some people become more cynical while others feel a sense of frustration or mounting anger.

The people who hire us think of the score we're writing as a compilation of chords, notes, instruments, technology and similar ingredients which we acquired knowledge of in school. They don't understand that part of what we do comes from somewhere magical, from inside, from a spark that allows us to create something beyond what our education has prepared us for.

They think of it as a craft, a trade. We must do the same. We must separate ourselves from the music. Separate our ego from the music.

Think of yourself as an interior designer. Designers must remain aware that they are not going to be living in the house they are designing. Someone else is going to be waking up every morning with *that* wall color.

Simply, it is not your score that you are writing.

Creativity, unbridled, can interfere with doing a good job of scoring. Defining the parameters of your score can be helpful in establishing a playing field or defining the boundaries of a playground on which your creativity can run wild. Just don't run out in the street.

ON THE GOOD AND BAD NEWS

The Good News is that, with technological advances, the opportunity to become a film composer is available to more people now than ever before.

The Bad News is that in the past 15 years the number of film and television composers has at least tripled.

The Good News is that now more colleges and universities are offering curricula in media music.

The Bad News is that they are turning out hundreds of composer wannabes every year, creating an ever-expanding community of composers looking for work and competing for the significantly fewer jobs that exist.

The Good News is that cable TV has greatly increased the number of channels and consequently the number of programs being broadcast.

The Bad News is that television advertisers who used to divide advertising dollars among three major networks are now trying to divide those dollars many more times in order to have a presence on more channels. Fewer dollars means lower production budgets for those channels that produce original programming.

The Bad News is that there is a huge random card when it comes to landing a job.

The Good News is that because there is this random aspect to hiring composers, you have just as much chance as everyone else. Regardless of experience and credits.

WHY FILMMAKERS LIKE THE MUSIC THEY LIKE

There is no actual answer to this but some insight can be gathered from another question: "At what time in your life did music have the most dramatic impact?"

I believe the most popular answer would be around puberty. The ages between 12 and 16. Music likely accompanied your first romantic kiss, your first heartbreak, the first feeling of freedom while cruising down the main drag on Saturday night with your friends. I find out the age of the filmmakers I'm about to meet so that I can determine what music was most popular when they were young teenagers. If nothing else, it gives us some songs and artists to talk about.

CHAPTER NINE

STORIES

Embedded in these stories from my colleagues are valuable insights into the workings of our profession. I know you will enjoy reading this chapter and hope that you come away with something that will help you get through those awkward moments in your career, when you start collecting stories of your own.

I am so grateful to my friends for providing these wonderful chronicles and allowing me to publish them here.

Enjoy.

JOHN BEAL

Eight is Enough, Vega$, Chicago Story, Laverne & Shirley

SPOTTING WITH A DIRECTOR: "Now, when the jet-engine boats come roaring around the island and start blowing things up...that's where I want the solo oboe to come in." I'm thinking, "Oh boy, very hip—an action scene scored emotionally, the singular voice of the inner man in battle—" But my creative reverie is interrupted when the director says, "But you'll have to ask him to play really, really loud because there is going to be a ton of explosions."

PRODUCERS WHO ONLY THINK THEY UNDERSTAND THE PROCESS: "It's only a three-minute piece, how long could it take to write and produce? I'll just sit right here and have a cup of coffee."

PRODUCERS WHO REALLY KNOW HOW TO COMMUNICATE: "I'd like it to sound more like the way yellow cardboard looks when it rains."

PRODUCERS WHO TRUST: The wonderful producer Mace Neufeld understands the process of composing and of trusting his composer to show up on the stand with quality music that works seamlessly with his film. But (before we had all the great samples and computers to do fully realized demos), one of his assistants demanded after the spotting session that he get to hear every note of every cue before we arrived on the scoring stage. Mace turned to me with a wink and asked, "John, what is your primary instrument other than the orchestra?" "Drums and percussion," I replied. He turned to his assistant and said, "Do you really want him to play the entire score on a snare drum?"

HORROR STORIES: "We know it's the morning of the orchestra session, but we made a bunch of changes to this slapstick piece. We changed the order of a lot of the gags and where the pie hits the face, and where the pratfalls are, but it really shouldn't affect you, because after we finished, it's really only a net change of one foot of film."

HORROR STORIES: Back in the day before computer tempo mapping, we used calculators and slaved over constant and variable click tracks to figure our synch. I stood on the podium one day after years of conducting cues to picture which never, ever were out of synch, thanks to the wonderful mentoring I received from Earle Hagen. This time, though, there was a music supervisor who hadn't hired me—I had been hired by the producer of the TV show. EVERY cue was off. Nothing lined up after the first few bars. I kept running out of music on every cue in rehearsal. Panic. Break out the calculator. Scratch your head with the editor. Question your sanity. Punt and conduct wild to picture with no clicks or streamers. It turns out this guy was nudging the click generator box up a frame or two every couple of beats while we rehearsed. Once we figured out what he was doing and got him busy on the phone during the session, everything went smoothly again.

AMIN BHATIA

Get Ed, Jane Goodall's Wild Chimpanzees, John Woo's Once A Thief, Iron Eagle II

ON COMMUNICATION: Producers can be a very nervous bunch who are anxious to be regarded as hip and cool. At the first spotting session of a series I asked them, "What about style?" and they responded, "Oh my god yes, it has to have style!"

ON CONTROL: Some directors are control freaks who do not trust their teams or the interactivity that can grow between them. On one of my first action features there were a lot of sound effects and dialogue and I was worried about where and how my score should integrate into it. The director dismissed my concerns and insisted on an almost wall-to-wall score.

"I want a melodic score that harkens back to the golden era of Tiomkin and Steiner," he told me. "Give me lots of melody and don't worry about dialogue and effects. I need your score to save my film. Don't bother talking to the other guys in dialogue and effects. Just give me lots of music and I'll personally make sure it's nice and loud."

With that kind of encouragement I went nuts and had a field day with all sorts of motifs and clever counterpoint. At the mix I was horrified to hear the score buried amidst sound effects, ambiences and additional dialogue. Songs had also been brought into play in every scene featuring a car radio, a bar, or a restaurant. Had I known this intent, I would have written my cues very differently. But the director had expressly forbidden any of us to talk to each other, and spotting sessions for each department were kept private from the other.

I found out later that he had told sound effects, "I want to feel the power of every combat machine on screen. To hell with what they're saying or what the score is doing." To the dialogue editor he had said, "This story is all about the characters. I want to hear every word and sentence clearly. Don't bother talking to the music guy or the sound effects team"…etc.

It was the director's way of getting each department to give him 110 percent so that he could pick and choose at the mix. Of course the result was a big loud mess. Because there was no forethought to the interactivity of score, effects and dialogue, there was no "orchestration" between the three.

Ironically and thankfully I've been asked to work with this director again and in subsequent films I insisted on communication between all departments. So we all learned from that experience, including him.

ON THE SEMANTICS OF TRUST: I was asked to write a demo cue for a scene in order to secure a sci-fi series. The scene involved a rescue between a virtual reality superhero trapped inside a computer and the boy from the outside world who saves him. The producers told me about friendship, camaraderie and loyalty between the characters. That is what they wanted the music to enhance, despite the computer sci-fi settings.

I spent days on several versions of cues which were contemporary and electronic while still maintaining a sense of friendship and pathos. I went out of my way with variable click tracks and hit points to wed the cue to the actions on screen.

The producers were very kind and impressed with the time I spent, but repeated review sessions made it clear that it wasn't working. We were just not speaking the same language. The cue "needs more" was all that they could communicate.

We finally gave up, shook hands and thanked each other for a valiant try. As we prepared to leave, the director dropped by to hear some music, and we told him that it just wasn't working out. The director asked "was it not desperate enough?"

In all the semantics used to describe what the cue needed, the producers had never used the word "desperate."

I asked if "desperate" meant "terror" or "panic" and they nodded. This was a very different direction, and another two days of cue demos felt quite daunting. But I had a DAT tape sitting nearby containing some frenetic African tribal cues I'd done for a cartoon show weeks before. I played a few seconds of that tape, which we ran manually alongside the scene and they shouted, "Eureka! That's it! Give us more of that stuff and you're hired!"

African drumming music for a sci-fi rescue scene was very unconventional but the energy of it worked perfectly to the scene. The show led to two other series and a high profile feature film all of which were handed to me carte blanche with no auditions. With that kind of trust and loyalty I was inspired to write all kinds of cues that challenged my musical abilities and delighted the producers. It was one of the most musically and personally enjoyable periods of my life.

Every now and then I stop to muse over the difference that ten seconds of a DAT tape made to three years of my career.

BRUCE BROUGHTON
Silverado, Tombstone, The Rescuers Down Under

WORKING WITH JERRY FIELDING: When I was working for CBS-TV, I was in the booth for a recording session with composer Jerry Fielding. Jerry, who was a terrific and highly skilled composer, was well known for his good days and bad days. One of the musicians asked about a note, "Jerry, is it E or E flat?" Jerry looked at the score and snarled, "I don't know. It doesn't matter. It's all shit, anyway." I looked at the score and thought, I'd like to write shit like this.

WORKING WITH MORT STEVENS: While working at CBS, I attended a spotting session for a TV movie with composer Mort Stevens, the composer of the *Hawaii Five-O* theme. At one point, the producer turned to him and said, "Now here, I'd like a horn." Mort, trying to maintain some creative control, turned to the producer and said, "Well that's an interesting idea. A French horn could make this scene sound very noble; although an English horn could make it sound very personal, if not a little oriental; while a basset horn might give the scene a very soft quality." The producer interrupted and said, "No, no, no. I mean a horn! You know, like Dizzy plays. A horn!"

WORKING WITH MICHAEL RITCHIE: I was recording the score to *A Simple Wish.* The director, Michael Ritchie, walked out to the stage to hear our 70-piece orchestra play one of the cues. As he walked back into the booth, he said, "I liked the synth version better."

WORKING WITH DON BELLISARIO: I had recorded a heavy love scene for a movie for director Don Bellisario. Don couldn't be there for the recording, so I played the scene back for him soon afterwards. Personally, I thought I'd nailed the scene with the very romantic music I had fashioned for it. He watched the picture and listened attentively to the playback. When it was all finished, he looked at me and said, "That's very romantic, Bruce. Very beautiful. Unfortunately," he continued, "the scene's not about love. It's about sex." I've told people this story before, and they always ask, "So what did you do? Add a sax?" Yep.

WORKING WITH BERNARD HERRMANN: Again I was in the booth at CBS when Bernard Herrmann was recording an episode of a western series, *Cimarron Strip*. At CBS, the orchestras were always 18 players, so Herrmann came up with an orchestra of six bass clarinets, six bassoons, and six double basses. "The highest note is middle C," he told everyone. And, typically, he wrote everyone in triads. The story was a Jack the Ripper story, so he went dark. And muddy.

The first cue was free-time, so he started conducting at the first streamer, but when it came to the final streamer, the orchestra still had a lot of music to play. So, the film was racked up again, and once more, the same thing: a good start, but a lousy ending. A third time, he did the same thing. Mort Stevens, the director of music for CBS and a good film conductor, was in the booth with me, laughing. "Look at that," he said. "He can't hit the streamer." So he got on the intercom and said to Herrmann, "Hey, why don't you come into the booth for one pass, and work on the mix. I can conduct one while you listen." Herrmann turned slowly around and looked into the booth. "What's the matter? Are you worried because I'm not hitting the last streamer? It doesn't matter. It's all going to work, anyway."

A month or so later, I asked the producer what he thought of the Herrmann score. "Incredible," he said. "The best score we had all year!"

THE FIRST RULE IN MAKING A SALE: I was working on a film and had written a song for it. The film was a small-budget picture, with a somewhat difficult production history and it had had money problems from the start. I had a morning meeting to play the demo for the director, and thought I'd made a good one. This was the first opportunity for the director to hear it. As I approached the editing room, I began to hear a loud and anguished voice from down the hall. As I walked into the room, the film editor was staring wide-eyed at the director who was on the other side of the room yelling into the phone. "What! Whattya mean? But that's impossible! I can't…" And so forth. After several minutes of this, the director slammed the phone down and stared painfully into space. "Hell, we've just lost our distribution!" It was black in the room and he looked absolutely lost. He looked around for a few seconds trying to gain some focus, and then saw me standing in the doorway with a tape cassette. "Lemme hear that song," he said. It never got into the movie.

INSTRUCTIONS: Before the movie *Tombstone*, I was instructed not to make it sound like a western. Before the movie, *Miracle on 34th Street*, I was told not to make it sound like a Christmas movie.

MARKETING: After I finished scoring *The Boy Who Could Fly*, the picture was screened for audiences with the title covered up. The studio execs were afraid that the title might give the story away.

THE VALUE OF FILM MUSIC: Soon after I had started working at CBS, right out of college, I was up in the CBS music library. The library had scores of classical works, as well as stock arrangements spanning decades in radio and TV and basically anything a network music department would need to do business. It was also the resting place for recorded TV scores.

I noticed a scratch pad of yellow paper that looked to have been made by having cut up manuscript paper and binding the sheets face down. The paper was cut into 3x4 pieces, and I noticed there was writing on the other side. I turned the top sheet over and recognized the handwriting. It had been a score by Jerry Goldsmith.

WORKING WITH ERNO NEUFELD, CONCERTMASTER: For years I worked on the TV show *Quincy*, composing most of the episodes for the series. *Quincy* was always recorded at Universal Studios and the concertmaster was always Erno Neufeld. Erno, who had had a stellar career as Universal's concertmaster before I was born, had been at the studio for years and years, had performed with all of the great film composers and had patiently put up with the arrival of many young, new guys like myself.

I could never impress Erno. Whatever I wrote, Erno would play... or correct. One time I wrote an arpeggiated pizzicato quadruple stop for the violins. "You can't play that," Erno said. "I saw it in Ravel," I said. "Not in that direction," he said.

So I made it my mission to get his attention. And finally, one day, I wrote something tricky enough that all of the violin players were scrambling over the part. Even Erno, I noticed, was gesturing at the music on his stand with his violin bow, conferring with his seat partner as I rehearsed the woodwinds and the brass, and the other violinists were working on their part. "I did it," I thought. "I finally got Erno."

The room at Universal was exceptionally dead and you couldn't hear much without your headset. As I worked with the other parts of the orchestra, I had my headset off so I couldn't hear any conversation from the strings, but all I could think of as I rehearsed everyone else was, "I got him. I finally got him." I proudly put on my headset, and, as Erno was still gesturing in the direction of the music stand, I heard him say, "Now this one will net you eight percent, but this one here will get you ten percent."

ALF CLAUSEN
The Simpsons

I had the pleasure of writing an original *Simpsons* song for the famous rock band U2. Bono, The Edge and the guys were set to sing my song on a voice-record session at the Fox Newman Stage.

Once the *Simpsons'* producers were finished recording U2 on the scripted lines for the show, it was my turn to record the vocals. The booth was filled with over 50 people, including U2's publicists, legal folks, the *Simpsons'* producers, PAs, publicists, legal folks and representatives from the FOX music and legal departments.

I started to rehearse U2 to the pre-recorded song track as my engineer Rick Riccio worked on getting the proper recording levels. We were finally ready to record. The excitement in the air was almost too much to bear.

We rolled tape and recorded the first take. It was sung quite well, but I held down the talk-back button and said to Bono, "That was pretty good, but I think we can do a better one!" You could hear the collective gasp of over 50 people as the air was being sucked out of the room. I'm sure those folks were all thinking at once, "This guy just told Bono that what he sang wasn't good enough! D'oh!"

Fortunately, Bono and the guys understand what it's like to record vocals in this manner to get the best possible performance down on tape. This is also the way they are accustomed to recording. They were very cooperative as we recorded each section of the song again and again until we got a version that we were all happy with. The final result was amazing, and we parted company at the end of the day with a newfound, mutual respect for one another.

The echoes of that collective gasp still reverberate in my subconscious. I don't think they will ever disappear. That day was one of the highlights of my composing and recording career.

JAMES DI PASQUALE
The Shell Seekers, Love Lives On, Two of a Kind, Uneasy Lies the Crown

Like most composers, I have always previewed my scores for producers and directors using whatever technology was currently available. But in the early 1980s, before MIDI, samplers, or computers, I had an experience that really taught me the psychology involved in the previewing process. I was scoring a TV movie starring Helen Hunt for two former agents who were producing their first film. The director was somewhat experienced, but had a reputation for being nervous when it came to dealing with music. So I decided to preview the score in as complete a form as I could, rather than to play the thematic material live on piano as I had been doing. My goal was to have absolutely no surprises for either the filmmakers or myself when we got to the scoring stage.

Using a VHS video print of the film, a portable stereo video recorder, and a 4-track audio tape recorder, I dubbed a mock-up of the score onto the extra track of the video recorder. This produced a mixed music track in total synch with the picture on the work print videotape. I then played the video for the filmmakers in the home of one of them. We looked at the entire picture and discussed each cue and its placement in the film. All three men appeared to love everything they heard. I left feeling content that I had their full approval of my score.

The next day, the director called. After some small talk, I asked if he had any further thoughts, comments, or ideas about the music he had heard and approved. "No," he said. Well, why the call then?

"I just want to stay involved," he said. I explained that, unless he wanted to help me orchestrate cues, there was nothing for him to do at this point but to show up at the scoring session in 10 days. That seemed to placate him and I went back to work.

Well, the scoring session was a nightmare: I had 47 musicians on the stage at CBS, 44 minutes of music to record in six hours, and the producers and the director had a debate about virtually every cue. It was as though they had never heard a note of the music beforehand. They kept repeating, "We didn't know it would sound like this." The three of them asked to hear cues with various sections of the orchestra taceted. They even had me record an eight-minute cue in four different versions, including one using only two guitars. I indulged them with as much patience as I could muster. Finally, the CBS music supervisor had had it: he pulled the three guys aside and said that for the rest of the session, we would record the music only as originally composed. Further, he lectured to them about the music budget, their inexperience, and what is possible in recording a music score. We then completed the session, going a half-hour overtime.

In the film dubbing session, the debates about the score started all over. The three filmmakers could hardly agree on anything. I found myself arguing mostly with the director who seemed to be completely insensitive to what the music was contributing to the film. Finally, the head dubbing engineer had enough: he lectured the filmmakers about how they were ruining the score, going over budget, and running out of time to finish dubbing their film. The director then left the room in a huff and the dub continued with virtual silence from the producers.

The film aired on CBS with most of my score in its original form. It received good numbers, was well reviewed, and the producers went on to have a fairly successful production company. Helen Hunt, of course, became a major star. The director, however, slowly disappeared from the business, a victim of his reputation for being difficult to work with.

As horrendous as the whole experience was, I learned a valuable lesson which I've never forgotten: no matter how complete the score mock-up, no matter how much approval you receive from filmmakers, when you get to the scoring and dubbing stages, a different reality takes over. The music is then heard in relative balance to dialogue and sound effects.

That often results in everything being reevaluated by nervous directors or producers who are fixated on the flaws in their film, and are now looking for music to solve all their problems. They may completely reverse the collective decisions made earlier and expect the composer to comply immediately. Often, it's a direction that you know will be less effective or, worse, disastrous for the film. This is especially true of inexperienced filmmakers, but it can happen to veterans, too. All the composer can do is protect and defend the original vision that was agreed upon. Beyond that, the film is ultimately the production team's baby to destroy; all too often, that's exactly what they do. The best that the film composer can achieve in this situation is to emerge as unscathed as possible, and hope that the next film results in a more positive scoring experience.

Fortunately, those experiences do exist, rare though they might be.

ADAM FIELDS
Dawson's Creek, Buffy the Vampire Slayer, Meeting Daddy

In the early 90s, I was lucky enough to be apprenticing for a talented TV and film composer, henceforth referred to as John Smith. His project at the time was a television movie, temped with music from a famous historical documentary.

John assigned me several cues to ghostwrite, and it was then that I contemplated the single most brilliant plan of my film-scoring career. I researched and found the names of the "specialty" musicians who played on that famous documentary. "What if…" I wondered, "…we got those same musicians to play on OUR score!?" It was too good to be true. "The director will LOVE us," I added, with the confidence only a 25-year-old with little experience could have.

"I'm not sure that's such a good idea," John responded to me after I brought him the idea.

He went on.

"Those musicians live in New York State. So you've got the expense of flying there, a hotel room, a studio you're not familiar with, and two musicians you only know from one documentary. It's a nice, 'romantic' idea, and creative, but it's not practical. We can get the same sound from local L.A. musicians."

But I was determined. If the director loved his temp score, he'd LOVE us for using those same musicians on his original score.

Fluffing off my mentor's advice, I packed my bags, enlisted the help of my engineering buddy Steve, and we boarded a plane bound for an unknown studio in upper New York State.

The studio, to our surprise, was fairly well-equipped, and the musicians were charming and friendly. So it was, therefore, a minor disturbance when we were informed that they couldn't really sight-read music. "Not that well, anyway," they said to me, clutching my stack of cues.

What followed in the 10 hours we had booked at that studio can only be described as an unmitigated disaster. We weren't getting anything close to the sound we needed for this film.

On a break, Steve took me outside, grabbed my shoulders and said: "We need to cut our losses and get out of here. We'll go back to L.A., we'll re-record, but we've got to leave now or we're throwing money away."

He was right. But the thought of returning home to my mentor with nothing in the can was too unbearable to consider. So we stuck out the rest of the day, recorded whatever we could, and hightailed it back to California.

To help fix and smooth over the New York cues, we ended up hiring some L.A. studio musicians anyway. And with the help of their perfect performances and some nifty editing, we actually squeaked by with some acceptable cues, and the director was satisfied.

John, my mentor, didn't have to say "I told you so." In fact, to this day, it occurs to me that part of his permission for me to go and try out my idea may have been to teach me the valuable lesson I now wish to impart to all of Richard's readers.

Here it is:

There's no place like home.

Without question, Los Angeles is home to the best studio musicians in the world. These are people who can sight-read any level of music with ease and skill. People who'll give you the best performances, on time, and on budget.

You may think you're saving money by going elsewhere. Another state, another country even. But think twice before considering such a move. Going local may end up actually saving you money in the end. Because the musicians always get it right. The first time. No plane trips. No hotel rooms. No risk.

They're the best, and they're worth every penny.

DAN FOLIART
7th Heaven, Home Improvement, Roseanne

It was in the Spring of 1988. My then partner, Howard Pearl, and I had been offered the fortuitous opportunity to meet with a young producer/writer from New York, Matt Williams. Gayle Maffeo, a talented producer in her own right, who had become a close personal friend, had arranged the interview in the Culver City area. She was starting to assemble the talent for a new series featuring an unknown comedienne, Roseanne Barr. Gayle had worked with us on a number of occasions and felt that we would be a good fit for this upcoming pilot for the proposed series.

Well, as it happens, we arrived at this meeting with a demo of a piece that we had completed after reading the script for "Roseanne." Matt was very polite, but also was quite demonstrative as he described how our slick dance-oriented theme was totally wrong for the show. Matt has always been spot on as far as describing what he wants and what he doesn't want for his shows. One thing was clear, he didn't care for this attempt. He began to describe the rural bluesy palette that we should be working in and a real profile for this character began to evolve. Even though we hadn't seen Roseanne up to this point, we understood the character and what needed to be achieved.

Well a few days passed, Howard and I wrote a new piece and I arranged to get six of L.A.'s most talented and inspired musicians into the studio, contrasting with the clinical, synthesized mock-up that had been rejected a few days earlier. Gary Herbig, Laurence Juber, John "Juke" Logan, Domenic Genova, John Beasley and Michael Jochum arrived at Sound City Studios on Cabrito Road in Van Nuys early on the morning of March 22nd with our engineer, Tim Boyle. The "rocked out" studio, known for sessions featuring Dylan, The Band and other such roots based groups was the perfect setting, and the stench from the previous late night pervaded the studio as we moved in. Those of you who know me would be surprised by the unshaven, jeans-clad shell of my former self who arrived in a ripped up T-shirt with a beat up Epiphone Texan guitar. It was with this persona that I walked into the room, and started strumming the opening chords to our new theme. Well, what transpired was decidedly more successful than our previous outing. Not only did we enlist Matt and the other principles involved, but what we came up with was the theme that lasted for the run of the series, though it was re-arranged a couple of times before the show ended in 1997. The point being, always listen—listen closely and when you've absorbed, do your best to set the proper stage for acceptance. ■

And now, one last story.
This one from my own vault:

RICHARD BELLIS
Stephen King's IT, Doublecrossed,
One Special Night, Malpractice

DISNEYLAND'S INDIANA JONES ADVENTURE: It's 4:00 a.m., I just got off work and I'm driving home. I'm bruised, nauseous and generally beaten up. Have I taken a second job as a nightclub bouncer to supplement my earnings as a composer? No, I have just come from the most violent spotting session of my life.

It was midnight when we arrived at "The Happiest Place On Earth." Ed Kalnins, Adam Fields and me—Team Bellis—The "A" Team (for "A"nal retentive). Here we were to attack the inevitable slew of problems that crop up in the course of embracing the bleeding edge of technology. We are honorary Imagineers, consultants to Walt Disney Imagineering, the organization that creates all the rides and attractions for Disneyland, Walt Disney World, Disneyland Resort Paris and Tokyo Disneyland.

The Indiana Jones ride was nearing completion. I was brought on board four months prior and since then had been involved in creative meetings, researching cues from John Williams' original scores, producing demos, riding prototypes and visiting the actual site for walks-through. The ride was the newest venture into simulator technology. It is essentially a motion base (a la Star Tours) mounted on what can only be described as a slot car track. The motion base is disguised as a desert terrain vehicle with three rows of seats, each row holding four passengers (or victims). One of the exciting musical features of this ride is that each row is equipped with five speakers used solely for music playback. This means that each rider has his/her own stereo pair. Because the layout of the five speakers is left channel, right channel, left, right, left, some people will have a reversed stereo image but hey, when you're being tossed around who cares what side the violins are on? Another first for this kind of high-tech roller coaster ride is that the music is scored, like a film, to recognize every important bounce, bump, and bang. In order to facilitate this, we had to "spot" the ride.

The first attempt at spotting was to make a videotape using a camera lashed to the vehicle and SMPTE code burned in. While this was of some help in putting together rough timings, it lacked two important features. First, you could not really get a sense of the vehicle bucking and pitching around. You could see it but not feel it. Second, these rides continue to be tweaked up until, and beyond, the date they are opened to the public. The videotape, consequently, became outdated within days of its creation. So, we selected a spotting deadline, backed in from the recording session. We would actually go on the ride with stopwatches akimbo and time the individual cues that would make up the continuous score.

We had broken the ride into about 10 cues. All cues had long tails in order to accommodate changing the moment that the next incoming cue would start. This would allow us a minimum amount of slip and slide (a few frames at most) with which to accommodate future tweaking. There were to be two versions of the ride, which meant that about four cues had to be timed twice, once in the "A" scenario and once in the "B". This then meant that we had 14 cues to time. Being the "anals" that we are, we knew we should time each one at least twice. Then came the proverbial fly in the ointment.

We were informed that the vehicles were incapable of reversing direction and that we would have to complete the full ride each time. Okay, so we have 28 timings (14 cues timed twice) and two stopwatches, two pencils and two legal pads. It stands to reason that if Ed and Adam time alternate cues while I sit between them and conduct starts and stops we should be done in four trips or so. Four rides at just over three minutes per ride, dare I utter the words that fill composers' hearts with overwhelming fear? Sure. "How long could it take?"

"Go," I confidently say as we start into the darkness. Darkness?! Okay, next time around we bring flashlights. We ascend the first ramp moving closer to Mara, the huge godhead with smoke emanating from her eyes. Adam is taking notes and squinting at his stopwatch. Ed is waiting for the turn to the left as we pass Mara. Here it comes...*Lurch!!* The legal pad jumps a foot off his lap but he manages to catch it. That's the good news. The bad news is that he didn't start his watch. All right, forget that one, we'll get the skeletons in the catacombs next. "Get ready...go!" Adam, who manages to start his watch, is frantically holding on to the stopwatch with one hand and the legal pad with the other, unable to write as we blaze through the catacombs. "Remember these times!" he shouts, "18 seconds, 22 seconds, 25 and a half." We jolt to a slowdown. Whew! Uncontrollable laughter, during which we miss the next timing. "All right, let's get the next one, here it comes...." the vehicle suddenly stops dead. This is not supposed to happen. Oh well, we'll chalk this first trip up to experience. Let's just get back to the start and try again. Fifteen minutes later we're still sitting in the middle of a suspension bridge while engineers are inspecting the track. They'd obviously done this before. They had flashlights.

By the 22nd time around, we were getting good. Good and bruised. The only thing that went wrong on our last trip was that my cell phone came loose from my belt and bounced several times on the floor, causing me to miss a downbeat. Had we known that night how much digital editing was in our future, we would have gone home after the eighth or ninth trip chanting: "We'll fix it in the editing."

What followed, of course, made the agony of the spotting session worth it. An 86-piece orchestra for an afternoon at Todd AO, playing what seemed like a medley of John Williams' chase cues. I think that at the end of the four-hour session, the string players felt much like we did after the spotting session.

The final step after mixing was to sample the cues, lash a keyboard (from which to trigger the samples) onto the vehicle and attempt to play each sample (cue) at the appropriate start mark as again, we encouraged the onset of chronic whiplash.

While working for Walt Disney Imagineering is always mentally and technically challenging, it is the physical demands put on me as composer that make me a regular at the gym. The rigors of writing music for the Tower of Terror, Alien Encounter, Star Tours and Indiana Jones Adventure makes one remember with tranquil affection The Hall of Presidents.

APPENDIX

SELECTED RESOURCES:

University of Southern California
Thornton School of Music
www.usc.edu/schools/music/programs/smptv

> *The USC campus is located in Los Angeles, home to many compos-*
> *ers, arrangers, filmmakers, musicians and studios. The USC Scoring for*
> *Motion Pictures and Television Program is a one-year intensive course*
> *of study. Students in this program spend many hours studying scores,*
> *screening films, composing music, producing recording sessions and*
> *learning from faculty and guests who are working professionals in the*
> *film music industry.*

UCLA Extension
www.uclaextension.edu

> *The UCLA Extension's Entertainment Studies and Performing Arts Film*
> *Scoring Certificate, created in 1984, was the first program of its kind. In*
> *this program, students compose and conduct their own scores in front*
> *of an orchestra and develop their composition, songwriting, and dra-*
> *matic interpretation skills under the direction of instructors who are*
> *working film composers.*

California State University, Northridge
www.csun.edu/music

> *CSUN's Commercial and Media Writing Option (B.M.), coordinated by*
> *Professor Elizabeth Sellers, is part of the university's Music Theory and*
> *Composition Department. Performance auditions are required for*
> *admission. Coursework includes songwriting, keyboard, music history,*
> *music recording, MIDI sequencing, composition, conducting, music*
> *industry studies, orchestration, private lessons and internships.*

The Society of Composers & Lyricists (SCL)
www.thescl.com

This is the largest trade organization in North America for film and television composers and lyricists. It is based in Los Angeles and is currently establishing a presence in New York. It offers many seminars, screenings and lectures, which are free to members and available to nonmembers for a fee. The SCL has a quarterly publication and a mentor program. The associate membership level doesn't require professional credits.

SCL Mentorship Program
The SCL's mentor composers are working film and television composers who volunteer their time and expertise to introduce interns to the profession of film scoring. During this three-month program, interns have the opportunity to meet with and observe the work of the music editor, orchestrator, music copyist, scoring engineer, orchestra conductor and performing musicians.

Shows observed as part of the program have included the Star Trek *series,* JAG, The Simpsons, 7th Heaven *and various films. The intern is mentored in orchestrating and composing practice exercises from the sessions observed.*

The Guild of Canadian Film Composers
www.gcfc.ca

The GCFC sponsors seminars and has a publication, an internship program and a unique and informative e-mail discussion list.

The GCFC Apprentice/Mentor Program
During the course of this six-week program, three separate terms are completed: one each in the regions of Vancouver, Toronto and Montreal. For each term, one selected apprentice is paired with one mentor film composer for an introduction to music-to-picture scoring in a 'real world' business environment.

ASCAP (American Society of Composers, Authors and Publishers)
www.ascap.com

ASCAP is a Performing Rights Organization (PRO) and sponsors two scoring workshops each year.

The ASCAP Television & Film Scoring Workshop with Richard Bellis:
Through a series of lectures, aspiring film and television composers in this program receive real-world knowledge and advice from industry executives, agents, attorneys, composers and studio musicians. Participants then have the opportunity to record an original composition on a major studio scoring stage, with a group of Hollywood professionals (including a 40-piece orchestra, a scoring mixer, composers and music editors) acting as coaches and mentors.

The NYU/ASCAP Foundation Film Scoring Workshop in Memory of Buddy Baker:
Held at NYU, this workshop is named in memory of Disney legend, ASCAP Foundation Lifetime Achievement Award winner and USC professor, Buddy Baker. The workshop covers the mechanics of timings and the art of composing music for picture. Participants have the opportunity to compose, orchestrate, conduct and record a cue with a professional ensemble. (Orchestras have included musicians from the New York Philharmonic and Metropolitan Opera Orchestra.)

BMI
www.bmi.com

BMI is a Performing Rights Organization (PRO) and sponsors many seminars and workshops throughout the year. The Composers Lab, co-sponsored by the Sundance Institute, is described on BMI's website.

Sundance Composers Lab
The Composers Lab is held each summer at the Sundance Institute. It is a major component of the Sundance Institute Film Music Program, which is dedicated to supporting emerging film composers and enhancing the role of music in independent film. The Composers

Lab provides valuable firsthand experience in composing for film and enhances the musical understanding of independent filmmakers participating in the Sundance Institute Feature Film Program.

BMI Conducting Workshop:
This free, annual workshop is designed for composers who want to refine their conducting techniques. Participation is limited to a selection of eight BMI-affiliated professional film and television composers. Using a repertoire from classical to commercial film music, participants work with live players—ranging from a piano duet to a full chamber orchestra. The curriculum includes conducting free form as well as to click track, with and without picture. Each session is videotaped and critiqued.

The BMI Foundation's Pete Carpenter Fellowship:
This annual fellowship is open to aspiring film composers under the age of 35. The successful candidate will have an opportunity to work for four to five weeks with Mike Post (composer of TV themes such as NYPD Blue, Hill Street Blues, L.A. Law *and* Law & Order), *meet with other distinguished theatrical, film, and television composers, and receive a $3,000 stipend for travel and expenses.*

Made in the USA